Y0-BSX-902

ISBN # 0-9664970-1-5

Published by C. Glory Publications
2775 Custer Drive
San Jose, CA 95124
1-877-527-8329

ACKNOWLEDGEMENTS

A deep appreciation and gratitude to my loving & understanding wife and family, who for almost ten years has put up with and assisted in my obsession in this study-turned writing- project. Also my grateful appreciation to Ross & Jean Bratt, Jay Eubanks, Ross Wilson, Carl & Debbie Budge, Dave Nowack, Steve Cox, and many, many others to whom I am very much indebted.

"..AND THERE SHALL BE SIGNS.."

THE EVENTS OF THE
2^(ND) COMING OF JESUS CHRIST

A SIMPLE LISTING AND GUIDE
TO ASSIST CHRISTIANS IN IDENTIFYING
KINGDOMS AND EVENTS
(THE "SIGNS OF THE TIMES")
LEADING UP TO THE
2^(ND) COMING OF JESUS CHRIST

by
Roger K. Young

"And there shall be signs in the sun, and in the moon, and in the stars; and upon the earth distress of nations, with perplexity; the sea and the waves roaring.

"And when these things begin to come to pass, then look up, and lift up your heads; for your redemption draweth nigh.

"So likewise ye, when ye shall see all these things, know that it is near, even at the doors.

"Verily I say unto you, This generation shall not pass till all these things be fulfilled.

"Watch ye therefore, and pray always, that ye may be accounted worthy to escape all these things that shall come to pass,..." [1]

---

[1] *Luke 21:25, 28, 36 Matt.24:33, 34*

"For yourselves know perfectly that the day of the Lord so cometh as a thief in the night.

"For when they shall say, Peace and safety; then sudden destruction cometh upon them, as travail upon a woman with child; and they shall not escape.

"But ye, brethren, are not in darkness, that that day should overtake you as a thief.

"Ye are all the children of light, and the children of the day: we are not of the night, nor of darkness.

"Therefore let us not sleep, as do others; but let us watch and be sober." [2]

"Watch therefore: for you know not what hour your Lord doth come."[3]

---

[2] *1 Thes .5:2-6*

[3] *Matt.24:42*

A PURPOSE

I have taught Sunday School for over twenty years. During that time, without a doubt, one of the most frequently requested subjects is the Second Coming of Jesus Christ. Everyone is concerned about it because they want to know what is coming and how it will affect them. After twenty years of teaching the subject, I have spent the last ten years trying to put my study/lessons into a book form to share with others beyond my small Sunday School classes.

We all read about the terrible judgements of God that are to come upon the earth in the last days, the days of God's justice against the wicked. To some, it would appear that many of the current events now happening around us are those very events which were long ago prophesied would come just prior to the promised Second Coming of Jesus Christ in power and glory. Others believe the prophetic word to one degree or another, but believe that the Coming is still many years away and therefore of no concern or consequence to them. There are also those who also believe, but, they are so very busy in the daily troubles and concerns of modern life that they just don't take the time to stop and consider. Besides, life...though hard and sometimes difficult, is generally good, so why worry? Still, many others dismiss the very same events with nary a second thought, passing them off perhaps as coincidence, or just a jumbled mass of old idle threats intended to scare ancient believers...anything but the fulfillment of the writings of ancient men inspired by God with the gift of seeing the future and describing these events to us...both as a means of demonstrating and testifying that Jesus is verily the Christ, the same who was crucified in ancient days and who is soon to appear in glory as promised, and as a means to help those who believe and are watching, to prepare themselves and their families in order to avoid much of the foretold calamities.

It is my belief that if one analyzes the Biblical word concerning these ancient prophecies, that there is a common consistency and order running throughout them. This brief study is an attempt to list these events in the order that the Bible suggests, analyzing them briefly, and then compare them to recent and current events. The result I think adequately speaks for itself...

I add my voice to the chorus that declare that the Lord Jesus is the Christ, and that His long prophesied coming is soon at hand. I also have written this to help encourage people to come unto Jesus and to begin their preparations, both spiritual and physical, in order to avoid much of the effects of the terrible events that await us in the near future. If I am successful with at least one individual in bringing them to Christ, and preparing them for the events to come, I would consider this book to be successful.

[Note: I use the special name of Jesus, Christ, Jesus Christ, Savior and Lord interchangeably as is done in the Bible.]

All underlinings and boldings are my own. Scriptures are italicized.
The standard King James version of the Bible is used because that is what I grew up with and love the most. However, all of the scriptures are referenced so that they can be easily looked up in any of the Bible versions that are available today.

CONTENTS

A PURPOSE v

CHAPTER I
CATCHING US UNPREPARED 1
   As A Thief In The Night 1
   The Parable of the Ten Virgins 3

CHAPTER II
IDENTIFYING THE INITIAL SIGNS
TO GET A BASIC TIME FRAME REFERENCE 7
   PART A: LAYING THE FOUNDATION WITH LUKE 21 7
      AN INITIAL TIMETABLE FOR THE SECOND COMING 9
   PART B: NEBUCHADNEZZAR'S DREAM 13
   PART C: DANIEL'S VISION OF THE FUTURE 16
   PART D: THE REVELATION OF ST. JOHN THE DIVINE 21
   CHAPTER SUMMARY 24
   GRAPH: JOHN'S VISION OF EARTH'S EXISTENCE 27

CHAPTER III
NATURE GONE WILD 28
   GENERAL PLAGUES 28
   WEATHER RELATED 28
   PESTILENCE/DISEASE 29
   EARTHQUAKES 30
   VOLCANOES 31
   WARS & RUMORS OF WAR 31
   SIGNS IN THE HEAVENS 32

CHAPTER IV
IDENTIFYING THE KINGDOM
THAT EVENTUALLY GATHERS THE
ARMIES TO ARMAGEDDON 36
   TWO OPPOSING KINGDOMS IN THE LAST DAYS 36
   IDENTIFYING THE KINGDOM OF CHRIST IN THE
      LAST DAYS 38

IDENTIFYING THE SPIRITUAL KINGDOM OF SATAN
  IN THE LAST DAYS 39
    Identifying a Significant Political Kingdom of the Last Days . . . 41
    Listing the Political Kingdoms 19 Identifying Traits 41
    The Second Kingdom Comes To Power 43
    Summary listing of these 19 identifying traits 45
NAMING A PARTICULAR POLITICAL COUNTRY 46
    Testing the Country For the 19 Identifying Traits 46
    Testing the Country for Possible Future Fulfillment of
      Traits 13-19 49
      ADDITIONAL SCRIPTURAL CONFIRMATION 55

CHAPTER V
THE SEVEN LAST PLAGUES
OF THE WRATH OF GOD 58
    Over View Discussion 58
    LAST PLAGUE #1 60
    LAST PLAGUE #2 61
    LAST PLAGUE #3 62
    LAST PLAGUE #4 63
    LAST PLAGUE #5:A STRANGE WAR...*THE FIRST "WOE"* 64
    LAST PLAGUE #6 MORE DEVASTATING WARS...
      THE SECOND "WOE" 67
      GEORGE WASHINGTON'S VISION OF A
        FUTURE DEVASTATING WAR IN AMERICA 69
      THE LAST BATTLE AT ARMAGEDDON 71
      MAP: ANCIENT KINGDOMS OF ARMAGEDDON 74
      MAP: ISRAEL, SHOWING MEGGIDDO 75
      THE ABOMINATION OF DESOLATION 76
      THE GREAT FALSE PROPHET & THE ANTI-CHRIST 77
      THE TWO PROPHETS OF JERUSALEM 81
    LAST PLAGUE #7 *THE BEGINNING OF THE THIRD AND*
      FINAL "WOE" 83
      A TREMENDOUS PLAGUE OF HAIL 86
      ALL LIFE IN THE SEA DIES 88
      THE SAVIOR'S APPEARING TO THE JEWS 89
      THE GREAT SUPPER OF THE GREAT GOD 91
      VOICES IN THE HEAVENS 93
      A NEW TEMPLE IN JERUSALEM, A NEW RIVER FLOWS . 94
        RED HEIFER CALF BORN IN ISRAEL 95

SUN DARKENED/MOON TURNED TO BLOOD/
STARS FALL FROM HEAVEN 98
NO DARKNESS AT NIGHTTIME 99
THE GREAT SIGN OF THE COMING OF THE SON OF MAN 99
THE HOLY CITY OF NEW JERUSALEM 100
THE RIGHTEOUS LIVING AND DEAD RISE TO HEAVEN 101
SILENCE IN HEAVEN 103
THE END OF THE 3RD WOE...When the Lord's Face Is
Revealed To The World 104
GRAPH: SUGGESTED TIMELINE OF EVENTS 112

CHAPTER VI
AND NOW...THE GOOD NEWS 113
Escaping the Terrible Events of the Last Days. 113

CHAPTER VII
CONCLUSION/SUMMARY 120

APPENDIX OF SUPPLEMENTAL REFERENCES 129
LOOKING AT SCRIPTURES FROM DANIEL 130
Daniel's Second Vision 130
Daniel's Third Vision 131
Daniel's Fourth Vision 133
THE PROPHET JOEL'S DESCRIPTION OF THE ARMAGEDDON
ARMY ATTACKING JERUSALEM/ISRAEL 136
OTHER INTERESTING NOTES FROM AROUND THE WORLD
THE EVIL KINGDOM OF THE BEAST Some Additional Current
Events For Consideration 140
National & Worldwide Citizen Registration Programs. 143
National Id Card and Citizen Registration Has Now Become New
Federal Law. 143
United Nations Taking over Sovereignty of the United States. . 143
U.N. Control over U.S. Military 144
U.S. Land Being Designated as U.n. Bio-reserve Areas 144
American Heritage Rivers Act 149
EPA 149
Economic Bondage & Depression 149
Promoting Immorality by the "State" 151
Y2K...The Millennium Bug 152

What Can You Do To Prepare 155
Survival Tips/Hints...Y2K Special Event Dates 156
WHITE BUFFALO, SIOUX PROPHECY HERALDING THE
MILLENIUM, IS BORN 161
THE "BIBLE CODE" 162
A Personal Note and Comment 164
INDEX 166

CHAPTER I

CATCHING US UNPREPARED

As A Thief In The Night

No one knows exactly when Jesus's coming will be, at least not the day nor hour of His coming. Jesus himself mentioned this fact over and over again, even going so far as to say that even the Angels in heaven didn't know.

> *"But of that day and hour knoweth no man, no, not the angels of heaven, but my Father only."* [1]

However, He did say that He would provide us signs, guideposts as it were, indicating the nearness of this glorious event as a means to testify that He was (and is) indeed the Christ, that His prophets/apostles spoke and prophesied as they were commanded to do, and as a way to help those who watch for these signs to prepare themselves and their families in order to avoid much of the tribulation associated with many of these events. Jesus likened these guideposts to watching for the signs indicating the nearness of summer.

> *"Now learn a parable of the fig tree; When his branch is yet tender, and putteth forth leaves, ye know that summer is nigh:*
> *"So likewise ye, when ye shall see all these things, know that it is near, even at the doors."* [2]

It is interesting to note that, in this example, the fig tree is one of the very last to bring forth its leaves at the very end of spring. In fact, it has been often used as the signal or "sign" that spring has passed and summer planting can be started.

---

[1] Matt 24:36

[2] Matt 24:32-33

The thing that should concern us most is that the Lord has said that His Coming will be *"as a thief in the night."*[1] **Indications are that Jesus's Coming will catch most people, including the very faithful, not ready.** The Bible states:

> *"Therefore be ye also ready: for in such an hour as ye think not the Son of man cometh."* [2]

It is generally accepted that the world at large will not be ready for the Lord's coming. The Lord himself said so:

> *"But as the days of Noe (Noah) were, so shall also the coming of the Son of man be.*
>
> *"For as in the days that were before the flood they were eating and drinking, marrying and giving in marriage, until the day that Noe entered into the ark,*
>
> *"And knew not until the flood came, and took them all away; so shall also the coming of the Son of man be."*[3]
>
> *"Likewise also as it was in the days of Lot; they did eat, they drank, they bought, they sold, they planted, they builded;*
>
> *"But the same day that Lot went out of Sodom it rained fire and brimstone from heaven, and destroyed them all."*
>
> *"I tell you, in that night there shall be two men in one bed; the one shall be taken, and the other shall be left.*
>
> *"Two women shall be grinding together; the one shall be taken, and the other left.*
>
> *"Two men shall be in the field; the one shall be taken, and the other left."*[4]

Besides the world in general, the Lord Jesus also indicated that His coming will catch many well-meaning Christians unprepared as well.

---

[1] *2 Peter 3:10*

[2] *Matt. 24:44*

[3] *Matt. 24:37-39*

[4] *Luke 17:28-29,34-36*

The Parable of the Ten Virgins

The parable of the 10 virgins, or the 10 followers of Christ (called Christians), brings this point out clearly. After discussing with His Apostles His second coming and the signs preceding it, the Lord then gave the parable:

> *"Then shall the kingdom of heaven be likened unto ten virgins, which took their lamps, and went forth to meet the bridegroom.*
>
> *"And five of them were wise, and five were foolish.*
> *"They that were foolish took their lamps, and took no oil.*
> *"But the wise took oil in their vessels with their lamps.*
> *"While the bridegroom tarried, they all slumbered and slept.*
> *"And at midnight there was a cry made, Behold, the bridegroom cometh; go ye out to meet him.*
> *"Then all those virgins arose, and trimmed their lamps.*
> *"And the foolish said unto the wise, Give us of your oil; for our lamps are gone out.*
> *"But the wise answered, saying, Not so; lest there be not enough for us and you: but go ye rather to them that sell, and buy for yourselves.*
> *"And while they went to buy, the bridegroom came;* ***and they that were ready went in with him to the marriage: and the door was shut.***
> *"Afterward came also the other virgins, saying, Lord, Lord, open to us.*
> *"But he answered and said, Verily I say unto you, I know you not.*
> ***"Watch therefore, for ye know neither the day nor the hour wherein the Son of man cometh."*** [1]

All of the virgins/Christians were expecting and waiting for the Lord to make his appearance. They all knew it was going to be soon. Some were completely ready (they had their lamps and oil), and some were only partially ready (with their lamps and some oil). The partially prepared had fallen into the Devil's trap of

---

[1] *Matt. 25:1-13*

thinking they would have enough time and warning just before the Bridegroom came to finish their preparations.

The Bridegroom tarried, or didn't come when first expected, and when it didn't happen immediately, as all expected, some of the waiting virgins still didn't finish their preparations, but all went to sleep. Now notice what happens. Things happened very quickly. The announcement was given *"Behold the Bridegroom cometh,"* catching them all by surprise and off guard and (this is the important part), before the partially prepared (termed foolish) could hurry and finish their preparations, it was too late, and they suffered the consequences of their inaction...**because of the speed at which events happened.**

Just before Jesus gave His disciples the parable of the ten virgins, He talked to them also about the good and evil servant. Here, both servants have been charged with the care of the Lord's household, to "give them meat," or to feed the members of the household the true word of God and watch over them. The good servant is one who, when the Savior's return comes unexpectedly and catches them by surprise, is still doing what he was supposed to be doing and then is well rewarded.

The evil servant is one who says in his heart *"My Lord delayeth his coming;"* and begins to *"smite his fellow servants, and to eat and drink with the drunken,"* or in other words he actually joins in the activities of the world he was supposed to protect his people from, even to the point of smiting/condemning/ridiculing his fellow servants who are still trying to keep themselves from the world, much like what the Apostles fought against after the death of Jesus. (See Jude:3,17-10; 2 Tim 3-4)   The Savior comes *"in a day when he looketh not for him, and in an hour that he is not aware of"* and then the evil servant is suitably rewarded for his actions along with the other hypocrites:

> *"Therefore be ye also ready: for in such an hour as ye think not the Son of man cometh.*
> *"Who then is a faithful and wise servant, whom his lord hath made ruler over his household, to give them meat in due season?*
> *"Blessed is that servant, whom his lord when he cometh shall find so doing.*
> *"Verily I say unto you, That he shall make him ruler over all his goods.*

4

> *"But and if that evil servant shall say in his heart, My lord delayeth his coming;*
>
> *"And shall begin to smite his fellowservants, and to eat and drink with the drunken;*
>
> *"The lord of that servant shall come in a day when he looketh not for him, and in an hour that he is not aware of,*
>
> *"And shall cut him asunder, and appoint him his portion with the hypocrites: there shall be weeping and gnashing of teeth."[1]*

Again it is a specific message to Christians everywhere that there will be too many who will declare in their hearts *"My Lord delayeth his coming"* and will be caught by surprise by the Lord's coming and will not be ready.

Again, no one knows the hour nor day of His coming, but we shouldn't really be worried about it. It appears from the Bible that if we haven't taken steps to become prepared before his actual coming, it will be too late. **The parable of the ten virgins brings out the need to worry and prepare for the events that occur several years just prior to His coming.**

There is strong evidence that we are now at exactly the point just before those events that will happen immediately before His Coming, which, when they do happen, will catch many so called Christians and most of the world off-guard because they have been thinking that His Coming is still a ways off, "slumbering" so to speak.

These extremely near, catastrophic predecessory events, which are perhaps at the most only a few years away, once started, will happen so fast that if we have not made adequate physical and spiritual preparations, we will not be able to do so. If we are prepared for those years prior to His Coming, we will be ready for Him when He does come. Those chaotic-becoming-catastrophic events during this time can be prepared for, and should be prepared for immediately.

As mentioned before, though no one knows the exact time of the Savior's Second Coming, Jesus himself, along with His Apostles and Prophets, said that they would give us a list of signs or events that would indicate the nearness of this glorious event. There is strong evidence that many of the great keys concerning this

---

[1] *Matt 24:44-51*

period of time immediately preceding the Second Coming of the Lord have fallen or are falling into place, and will soon begin to fulfill their final parts in the prophecies of the Last Days.

All of this together adds a lot of credence to the suggestion that the Second Coming is much, much closer than most of us actually want to believe. In addition, because Jesus' Coming is so close, we can probably identify most of the general scenario that leads up to it. Events are moving at a very rapid pace now and seem to be accelerating even more.

CHAPTER II

IDENTIFYING THE INITIAL SIGNS TO GET A BASIC TIME FRAME REFERENCE

PART A: LAYING THE FOUNDATION WITH LUKE 21

For those who stop and take the time to consider the words of the ancient Prophets and Apostles, there should be no doubt that we are in the very last days just prior to the return to the earth of our Lord and Savior Jesus Christ. When He was upon the earth during His mortal ministry, Jesus taught His disciples that He would die and be gone from the earth for a time... but, that He would return again, this time not as a normal mortal man, but in the clouds of heaven with Power and great glory, as the true God of this earth.

> *"For as the lightning cometh out of the east, and shineth even unto the west; so shall also the coming of the Son of man be.*
> *"...and they shall see the Son of man coming in the clouds of heaven with power and great glory."*[1]

> *"And when he had spoken these things, while they beheld, he was taken up; and a cloud received him out of their sight.*
> *"...this same Jesus, which is taken up from you into heaven, shall so come in like manner as ye have seen him go into heaven."*[2]

However, there are those who might lead us to believe that the Second Coming of the Savior has already occurred and that He is even now walking among us as a mortal man, similar to when He was first upon the earth. The Bible is very

---

[1]*Matt 24:27, 30*

[2]*Acts 1:9,11*

specific that this would not be the case when he returned again.   In fact Jesus himself warned us to not be deceived in the last days by this very argument:

> *"And he said, Take heed that ye be not deceived: for many shall come in my name, saying, I am Christ; and the time draweth near: go ye not therefore after them."* [1]

> *"Then if any man shall say unto you, Lo, here is Christ, or there; believe it not.*
> *"For there shall arise false Christs, and false prophets, and shall shew great signs and wonders; insomuch that, if it were possible, they shall deceive the very elect.*
> *"Wherefore if they shall say unto you, Behold, he is in the desert; go not forth: behold, he is in the secret chambers; believe it not.*
> *"For as the lightning cometh out of the east, and shineth even unto the west; so shall also the coming of the Son of man be."* [2]

This glorious dramatic Second Coming of Jesus has been foretold by almost all of the ancient prophets since the beginning of recorded history.   Isaiah, Ezekiel, Amos, Daniel, Moses, Jeremiah, Micah......all prophesied concerning this dramatic and earth shattering event.   Many expressed the desire to be there.   One might ask, why would this be-- considering that it would be a time of tremendous judgements unleashed upon the world?   Simply, because it will be the time when the devil...adversary of all righteousness...who, for six thousand years has been allowed to test and torment man, will finally be cast out with those who would follow him.   (See Rev 20:1-3) It will be the time when He whose eternal right it is to reign will come and rule over the earth for a thousand years as the true King of Kings and Lord of Lords, ushering in a time of peace and prosperity heretofore unknown by mankind.

It needs to be understood that it will not be governments, nor the policies and armies of men, who will bring this millennial peace upon the earth, but the return of Jesus Christ, the Messiah and Savior of the world, to the earth as its rightful ruler.   At this time all the inhabitants of the earth will bow the knee and

---

[1] *Luke 21:8*

[2] *Matt. 24:23-24,26,27*

8

acknowledge that Jesus is indeed the very Christ.

AN INITIAL TIMETABLE FOR THE Second Coming

Jesus, as He was teaching His disciples concerning this long foretold and marvelous event, which was to be foreshadowed by the destruction of the second Jewish temple, was asked later by His Apostles and close disciples to give them more detail concerning it. As this is recorded in the 21st Chapter of Luke, we appear to get an initial timetable of events that will precede the Savior's Second Coming. According to Luke:

> *"And they asked him, saying Master, but when shall these things be? and what sign will there be when these things shall come to pass?"* [1]

Jesus then tells them to not be deceived about false Christs, wars, earthquakes, pestilences, etc... the signs associated with His return. "But before all these" (Luke 21:12) things happened, several other events would happen first.

1. The Apostles/disciples will suffer great persecution and even death:

> *"...they shall lay their hands on you, and persecute you, delivering you up to the synagogues, and into prisons, being brought before kings and rulers for my name's sake.*
> *"And ye shall be betrayed both by parents, and brethren, and kinsfolks, and friends; and some of you shall they cause to be put to death." (See Luke 21:12-16)*

2. Jerusalem, Judea and the temple would be destroyed.

> *"And when ye shall see Jerusalem compassed with armies, then know that the desolation* [destruction of Jerusalem and the Temple] *thereof is nigh."* At this time, He tells them;
> *"let them which are in Judea flee to the*

---

[1] *Luke 21:7*

9

*mountains; and let them which are in the midst
of it* [Judea/Jerusalem] *depart out; and let not
them that are in the countries*[outside of Judea]
enter thereinto." Because, *" For these be the
days of vengeance, that all things which are
written may be fulfilled." (See Luke 21:20-22)*

**3. The Jews would be destroyed and scattered as captives into
all nations**.   Christ laments concerning those who would have
trouble in fleeing:

*"Woe unto them that are with child, and to
them that give suck, in those days! for there shall
be great distress in the land, and wrath upon this
people. And they shall fall by the edge of the
sword, and shall be led away captive into all
nations." (See Luke 21:23-24)*

**4. Jerusalem would be controlled by the Gentiles (the non-
Jewish), for a period until a specific time was over or fulfilled.**

*"...and Jerusalem shall be trodden down of the
Gentiles, until the times of the Gentiles be
fulfilled." Luke 21:24*

5. At the end of the time when the *"times of the Gentiles are fulfilled,"*
**or when the Jews would again control Jerusalem, there will be new
signs in the sun, moon, stars... the seas and waves would be roaring;
The nations of the earth would be in distress; men's hearts would be
failing them for fear of those things which are coming.**

*"And they asked him, saying, Master, but when shall these
things be? and what sign will there be when these things shall
come to pass?*
*"And he said, Take heed that ye be not deceived: for many shall
come in my name, saying, I am Christ; and the time draweth
near: go ye not therefore after them.*

*"But when ye shall hear of wars and commotions, be not
terrified: for these things must first come to pass; but the end is*

10

not by and by.

"Then said he unto them, Nation shall rise against nation, and kingdom against kingdom:

"And great earthquakes shall be in divers places, and famines, and pestilences; and fearful sights and great signs shall there be from heaven.

"And there shall be signs in the sun, and in the moon, and in the stars; and upon the earth distress of nations, with perplexity; the sea and the waves roaring;

"Men's hearts failing them for fear, and for looking after those things which are coming on the earth: for the powers of heaven shall be shaken.

"And then shall they see the Son of man coming in a cloud with power and great glory." (Luke 21:7-11, 25-27)

6. After these signs the world together will see Christ come through the heavens towards the earth:

"... the powers of heaven shall be shaken. And then shall they see the Son of man coming in a cloud with power and great glory." (Luke 21:26-27)

7. To conclude His teaching session and answer the question of *"when shall these things be?"* the Savior said that *"when these things begin to come to pass, then look up, and lift up your heads; for your redemption draweth nigh."* [1] This appears to be a reference that when these final signs begin to appear, then His coming is very near. He then speaks the parable of the fig tree about watching for the signs of summer to know when His return draws nigh, saying that in the generation that the signs are brought forth, indicating the nearness of His return (as in the example of the parable of the fig tree), all of the prophesied events will occur before that generation all passes away.

"And he spake to them a parable; Behold the fig tree, and all the trees;

---

[1]*Luke 21:28*

11

"When they now shoot forth, ye see and know of your own selves that summer is now nigh at hand.

"So likewise ye, when ye see these things come to pass, know ye that the kingdom of God is nigh at hand.

"Verily I say unto you, This generation shall not pass away, till all be fulfilled." [1]

8. He then finishes by telling them to be careful not to become too involved in the cares and activities of the world to the point of forgetting His coming. He then commands them to watch for the signs and pray so that they might be worthy to escape the terrible things which will come to pass.

"And take heed to yourselves, lest at any time your hearts be overcharged with surfeiting, and drunkenness, and cares of this life and so that day come upon you unawares.

"For as a snare shall it come on all them that dwell on the face of the whole earth.

"Watch ye therefore, and pray always, that ye may be accounted worthy to escape all these things that shall come to pass, and to stand before the Son of man."   (Luke 21:34-36)

{The version in Matthew 24 has even more detail concerning this question and answer session between the Savior and His disciples though the timing isn't as clear. This will be added in and discussed later in the book. See also Mark 13}

Matthew records that the Savior spent some time and effort to get the point across to His disciples concerning how important it was to keep watching and to be ready. He provided several parables to illustrate the point. These include the parable of the goodman and the thief (Matt 24:42-45), the parable of the faithful and wicked servant (Matt 24:44-51), the parable of the 10 virgins (Matt 25:1-12,

the parable of the talents (Matt 25:14-30), and the parable of the goats and sheep (Matt 25:31-46) which includes the quote; *"Inasmuch as ye have done it unto one of the least of these my brethren, ye have done it unto me."*

---

[1]*Luke 21:7-11, 25-27, 31-32*

If we start with this basic timetable as found in Luke (some of which has happened already), and add in the timetable reference as found in Daniel's interpretation of the dream of king Nebuchadnezzar, it seems to clarify the basic timetable even further. Let us take a minute to become acquainted with Necuchadnezzar's dream and Daniel's first vision.

PART B: NEBUCHADNEZZAR'S DREAM

Let us review the dream and the interpretation as given by God to Daniel and subsequently to king Nebuchadnezzar.

> *"And in the second year of the reign of Nebuchadnezzar, Nebuchadnezzar dreamed dreams, wherewith his spirit was troubled, and his sleep brake from him.*
>
> *"Then was the secret revealed unto Daniel in a night vision. Then Daniel blessed the God of heaven.*
>
> *"Daniel answered and said, Blessed be the name of God for ever and ever: for wisdom and might are his:*
>
> *"And he changeth the times and the seasons: he removeth kings, and setteth up kings: he giveth wisdom unto the wise, and knowledge to them that know understanding:*
>
> *"He revealeth the deep and secret things: he knoweth what is in the darkness, and the light dwelleth with him.*
>
> *"I thank thee, and praise thee, O thou God of my fathers, who hast given me wisdom and might, and hast made known unto me now what we desired of thee: for thou hast now made known unto us the king's matter.*
>
> ***"Thou, O king, sawest, and behold a great image. This great image, whose brightness was excellent, stood before thee; and the form thereof was terrible.***
>
> ***"This image's head was of fine gold, his breast and his arms of silver, his belly and his thighs of brass,***
>
> ***"His legs of iron, his feet part of iron and part of clay.***
>
> ***"Thou sawest till that a stone was cut out without hands, which smote the image upon his feet that were of iron and clay, and brake them to pieces.***
>
> ***"Then was the iron, the clay, the brass, the silver, and the***

gold, broken to pieces together, and became like the chaff of the summer threshingfloors; and the wind carried them away, that no place was found for them: and the stone that smote the image became a great mountain, and filled the whole earth.

"This is the dream; and we will tell the interpretation thereof before the king.

"Thou, O king, art a king of kings: for the God of heaven hath given thee a kingdom, power, and strength, and glory.

"And wheresoever the children of men dwell, the beasts of the field and the fowls of the heaven hath he given into thine hand, and hath made thee ruler over them all. ***Thou art this head of gold.***

"And after thee shall arise another kingdom inferior to thee, and another third kingdom of brass, which shall bear rule over all the earth.

"And the fourth kingdom shall be strong as iron: *forasmuch as iron breaketh in pieces and subdueth all things: and as iron that breaketh all these, shall it break in pieces and bruise.*

"And whereas thou sawest the feet and toes, part of potter's clay, and part of iron, ***the kingdom shall be divided*** *but there shall be in it of the strength of the iron, forasmuch as thou sawest the iron mixed with miry clay.*

"And as the toes of the feet were part of iron, and part of clay, so the kingdom shall be partly strong, and partly broken.

"And whereas thou sawest iron mixed with miry clay, they shall mingle themselves with the seed of men: but they shall not cleave one to another, even as iron is not mixed with clay.

"And in the days of these kings shall the God of heaven set up a kingdom, which shall never be destroyed: and the kingdom shall not be left to other people*, but it shall break in pieces and consume all these kingdoms, and it shall stand for ever.*

"Forasmuch as thou sawest that the stone was cut out of the mountain without hands, and that it brake in pieces the iron, the

brass, the clay, the silver, and the gold; the great God hath made known to the king what shall come to pass hereafter: and the dream is certain, and the interpretation thereof sure."[1]

Daniel says that there would be four kingdoms starting with the Kingdom of Babylonia. He says that at the end of the fourth kingdom, ten kings would come, described as *"feet and toes, part of potter's clay, and part of iron..."* and during their time the kingdom of God would be set up which would never be destroyed. The interpretation of the dream is generally as follows:

◆The 1st Kingdom/head of gold was King Nebuchadnezzar/Babylonia (6255-539 B.C.).[Daniel 2:38]

◆The 2nd Kingdom/breast and arms of silver (inferior to the first kingdom or Babylon), was the Medes and Persians Empire (539-331 B.C.).

◆The 3rd kingdom/belly and thighs of brass which would rule over all the earth, was the Macedonian or Greek Empire (331-161 B.C.).

◆The 4th kingdom/legs of iron which would break in pieces and subdueth all other kingdoms, was the Roman Empire. (161 B.C.-430 A.D.) Interestingly enough, later around 395 A.D., the Roman Empire broke apart with two capitals, one in Rome and the other in Constantinople corresponding to the two legs of the statue. (Later, the Catholic Church also broke into two similar parts now known as the Roman Catholic and the Greek Orthodox.)

◆Then a 5th kingdom/toes & feet of iron mingled with clay would come from the 4th kingdom after it was divided, the ten toes representing the ten major kingdoms of Europe[2] that would come to be after the downfall and breakup of the Roman empire. (The beginning of the breakup of the Roman Empire was around 467 A.D., leaving the last remnant of the Roman Empire which was called The Holy Roman Empire, centered in

---

[1] *Daniel 2:1, 19-23,31-45*

[2]*The subject of the ten toes and what kingdoms are represented has been discussed and disputed for almost 2000 years. It is my opinion that it is Europe. There are several reasons, most convincing is that it fits all of the criteria, including the point John says that it is from these that the Kingdom of the Beast comes from, which is discussed later. Also, it is from the European area that the Renaissance and the Christian spiritual rebirth (both in the 1500s and later in the 1800's) came from. The formation of Europe from 400 A.D. until the 1800's and even until now, is aptly described by saying it was divided, partly strong and partly broken, they shall not cleave one to another, etc.*

Germany. This lasted until the early 1800's when the modern nations of Europe started coming into being.)

The timing would seem to indicate that sometime after Europe was established a special resurgence and belief in Christ would come forth. This spiritual kingdom of God would come forth apparently after the establishment of the base 10 kingdoms of Europe. (It is interesting to note that the Protestant revival, with such great spiritual men as Martin Luther and others, began at this time and was centered in what was to become modern Europe, and led to the founding of America. Later, after the formation of the modern 10 kingdoms of Europe in the early 1800's, there was another further spiritual revival that seemed to affect all Europe and the United States.) Accordingly, then, the Savior's coming would be after the foundation of modern day Europe.

PART C: DANIEL'S VISION OF THE FUTURE

Daniel's First Vision

Daniel also had four visions wherein he saw future kingdoms, represented by beasts coming forth upon the earth. In the first vision, it describes a succession of four kingdoms symbolized by a lion, a bear, a leopard, and the fourth beast, the most terrible and strongest, which had ten horns. There are several similarities between this vision and the dream of Nebuchadnezzar, specifically concerning the fourth beast and the ten kingdoms that come from it. However, in this dream about these ten kingdoms, in addition to seeing a kingdom of God that is given to the saints of God for a kingdom forever, Daniel sees a terrible kingdom of evil that also comes forth from the ten kings/Europe and is eventually destroyed after 3 ½ years. The angelic person who destroys this evil kingdom is referred to as *"the Ancient of days"* and appears to be God who judges all things. God then gives the *"greatness of the kingdom under the whole heaven"* to the saints of the most high for *"an everlasting kingdom."* Again, no one knows for sure of the interpretation, and Daniel asked for the interpretation of only the fourth kingdom, but it is generally thought to be as follows...

1. The First beast...the Babylonian empire (Daniel 7:4)

> *"The first was like a lion, and had eagle's wings: I beheld till the wings thereof were*

plucked, and it was lifted up from the earth, and made stand upon the feet as a man, and a man's heart was given to it."

This easily could refer to the humbling process (plucking of wings) that Nebuchadnezzar experienced. Daniel's visions and dreams seem to all start with a common reference point, that of the kingdom in which he was a captive, that of Babylonia and later, Persia.

2. The Second beast...the Persian Empire (Daniel 7:5)

"And behold another beast, a second, like to a bear, and it raised up itself on one side, and it had three ribs in the mouth of it between the teeth of it: and they said thus unto it, Arise, devour much flesh."

This seems to fit the Persian Empire because its conquests were much greater than any predecessor kingdom, including the Asyrian, Babylonian, and Egyptian kingdoms.

3. The Third beast...the Greco-Macedonian Empire (Greece) (Daniel 7:6)

"After this I beheld, and lo another, like a leopard, which had upon the back of it four wings of a fowl; the beast had also four heads; and dominion was given to it."

This fits Greece because, after the death of Alexander the Great in 323 B.C., the Empire was divided among his generals into four sections. The Ptolemaic Empire, The Selecucid Empire, the Macedonian Empire, and Greece.

4. The Fourth beast...The Roman Empire (Daniel 7:7-8,19-27)
Note the similarities to the description of the Roman empire/kingdom/beast of

17

Nebuchadnezzar's dream. Including the ten horns/kingdoms which come from this "iron" kingdom.

"After this I saw in the night visions, and behold a fourth beast, dreadful and terrible, and strong exceedingly: and it had great iron teeth: and it devoured and brake in pieces, and stamped the residue with the feet of it: and it was diverse from all the beasts that were before it; and it had ten horns.

"I considered the horns, and, behold, there came up among them another little horn, before whom there were three of the first horns plucked up by the roots: and, behold, in this horn were eyes like the eyes of man, and a mouth speaking great things."

"Then I would know the truth of the fourth beast, which was diverse from all the others, exceeding dreadful, whose teeth were of iron, and his nails of brass; which devoured, brake in pieces, and stamped the residue with his feet;

"And of the ten horns that were in his head, and of the other which came up, and before whom three fell; even of that horn that had eyes, and a mouth that spake very great things, whose look was more stout than his fellows.

"I beheld, and the same horn made war with the saints, and prevailed against them;

"Until the Ancient of days came, and judgment was given to the saints of the most High; and the time came that the saints possessed the kingdom.

"Thus he said, The fourth beast shall be the fourth kingdom upon earth, which shall be diverse from all kingdoms, and shall devour the whole earth, and shall tread it down, and break it in pieces.

"And the ten horns out of this kingdom are ten kings that shall arise: and another shall rise after them; and he shall be diverse from

the first, and he shall subdue three kings.

"And he shall speak great words against the most High, and shall wear out the saints of the most High, and think to change times and laws: and they shall be given into his hand until a time and times and the dividing of time.

"But the judgment shall sit, and they shall take away his dominion, to consume and to destroy it unto the end.

"And the kingdom and dominion, and the greatness of the kingdom under the whole heaven, shall be given to the people of the saints of the most High, whose kingdom is an everlasting kingdom, and all dominions shall serve and obey him."

Again, from the ten kingdoms, or Europe, another kingdom would come forth, diverse from the rest, and shall subdue three kings, speak great words against God/Christ, persecute the "saints" (an early name for Christians used frequently in the Bible), and seek to change time and laws. But his kingdom/power shall be taken away after *"a time and times and the dividing of time,"* which again is often interpreted as 3 ½ years.

(Note: Daniel's last three visions are not discussed here, but are discussed in some detail in the Appendix.)

SUMMARY OF DANIEL

From Daniel, specifically Nebuchadnezzar's dream and Daniel's first vision we learn of a basic chronology of the world, from Daniel's time of approximately 600 B.C. forward to the end of the world. Both indicate the importance of the fourth kingdom and the ten kingdoms that come from it. Of course, after the Roman Empire a group of ten kings/kingdoms, both weak and strong, come forth, which have been identified as the forerunners of modern day Europe.

Also from Daniel we learn that apparently after these ten successor kingdoms to the old Roman Empire were established between 1500-1870 A.D., two opposing kingdoms would come forth. A kingdom of evil, which would initially come from among the nations of Europe and start out as a political or worldly kingdom, and another spiritual kingdom of God that is not a political kingdom and begins to gain strength after the ten kingdoms of Europe are formed. Though persecuted greatly by the evil kingdom, this spiritual kingdom of God would eventually inherit the earth when Christ comes the second time and destroys the evil kingdom.

As mentioned previously, at least a good part of the fulfillment of this spiritual kingdom of God coming forth could possibly be the great Christian spiritual revivals which began in the old remnants of the Roman Empire (called the Holy Roman Empire 962–1806 A.D.) under Luther and several others starting around 1500 A.D. spreading across the world, with the beginning of the last great spiritual revival in the 1800's.

The question then becomes, if this is all true, can we possibly identify the opposing evil kingdom that would come from Europe in the 1800's? And the answer is, probably. But first we need to gather more information from the scriptures.

---

[1]*The basis of these ten kingdoms could be argued to have come into being even as early as 1000 A.D. By 1190 A.D. the Roman Empire had divided up into the following general areas: France, England, Spain, Germany, Italy, Hungary, Poland, Bohemia (Czechoslovakia), Byzantine Empire (Greece), and Turkey.*

PART D: THE REVELATION OF ST. JOHN THE DIVINE

Several of the Apostles also wrote concerning some of the signs that would herald the nearness of the return of Jesus... providing us with additional details and information to help us identify and thereby recognize the signs of the Savior's return. The most prominent of these was the writing of the beloved Apostle John, also later called John the Revelator, the same who sat next to the Savior during the Last Supper.

While upon the isle of Patmos, John had a special vision that was in two general parts. The first, comprising chapters 1-3, contain special messages for the seven churches that were then in existence. The next part, starting with chapter 4, is primarily a vision of the history of the earth summarized into seven chapters in a book, with each chapter in the book sealed with a special seal. John is then allowed to view each of these chapters and briefly describe what he sees there. The first five chapters are very brief, sometimes covering a thousand years with just a few verses, but then there is much more detail concerning the end of chapter six and the beginning of chapter seven.

Chapter 1, the first "seal" was apparently a period of great war.

> *"And I saw, and behold a white horse: and he that sat on him had a bow: and a crown was given unto him: and he went forth conquering, and to conquer."* [1]

Chapter 2, the second "seal" was apparently a period of great bloodshed with no peace.

> *"And when he had opened the second seal, I heard the second beast say, Come and see.*

> *"And there went out another horse that was red: and power was given*

---

[1]*Rev 6:2*

to him that sat thereon to take peace from the earth, and that they should kill one another: and there was given unto him a great sword." [1]

Very little information concerning the first two thousand years, or 'seals,' of the earth's existence remains. The record found in Genesis seems to correspond to these first two seals in that it records that *"the wickedness of man was great in the earth, and that every imagination of the thoughts of his heart was only evil continually...The earth also was corrupt before God, and the earth was filled with violence."* [2] In fact God decided to destroy the inhabitants of the earth with a flood because *"it was corrupt; for all flesh had corrupted his way upon the earth...the earth is filled with violence through them;"* [3]

Chapter 3, the third "seal" suggests that perhaps it was a period of great famine.

"And when he had opened the third seal, I heard the third beast say, Come and see. And I beheld, and lo a black horse; and he that sat on him had a pair of balances in his hand.

"And I heard a voice in the midst of the four beasts say, A measure of wheat for a penny, and three measures of barley for a penny; and see thou hurt not the oil and the wine."

During this time period the Bible records the stories of three men and their families, wherein tremendous famines play a pivotal role in each of their lives. After the flood we have the story of Abraham. In Genesis it records that*"there was a famine in the land: and Abram went down into Egypt to sojourn there; for the famine was grievous in the land."* [4] During the life of Isaac there is a record of another famine [5] and about 100 years later, during the time of Jacob (also called Israel), another great famine was recorded. It is here where we have the story of

Joseph (son of Jacob) in Egypt in which He prepares Egypt for a famine that lasts

---

[1] *Rev 6:3,4*

[2] *Gen 6:5,11*

[3] *Gen 6:12-13*

[4] *Gen 12:10*

[5] *Gen 26:1*

for seven years. *"And there was no bread in all the land; for the famine was very sore."* [1]

Chapter 4, the fourth "seal" indicates that 1/4 of the population of the earth were killed by famine, war, disease, etc.

> *"And when he had opened the fourth seal, I heard the voice of the fourth beast say, Come and see.*
> *"And I looked, and behold a pale horse: and his name that sat on him was Death, and Hell followed with him. And power was given unto them over the fourth part of the earth, to kill with sword, and with hunger, and with death, and with the beasts of the earth."* [2]

Six hundred years later, we read in the story of Moses that, as a prince of Egypt, he went forth conquering, and then, later, of the great plagues that were visited upon Egypt in order to convince Pharaoh to let the descendants of Jacob/Israel go. Forty years later, the children of Israel conquered all of Canaan. After that, it appears to be a period of war and famine interspersed with a few years of peace, most notably during the reign of Solomon. After Solomon, Israel became extremely wicked, and in 1 Kings we read that Elijah sealed the heavens for many years so that drought and famine consumed the wicked. His successor, Elisha, also continued the drought/famine and records multiple wars, and later, another seven year famine. It is interesting to note that whereas Canaan, at the beginning of this period, was a lush land flowing with milk and honey, because of wickedness (Prophesied earlier by Moses. See Deuteronomy Chapters 27,28,29) it was visited continually with drought, famine and war so that by the end of this period it had become a barren land of desolation as had been prophesied by Moses.

---

[1] *Gen 47:13*

[2] *Rev 6:7,8*

Chapter 5, the fifth "seal" indicates that it was a period of great martyrdom for those who had a testimony of God.

> *"And when he had opened the fifth seal, I saw under the altar the souls of them that were slain for the word of God, and for the testimony which they held."* [1]

One of the great historical records was of the tremendous persecution of the early Christians, first by the Jews, and then by the Romans.

Chapter 6, the sixth "seal" is where things get very interesting and there is a lot more detail provided concerning the events.

John briefly lists five major events of the last days that he later describes in more detail.

> *"And I beheld when he had opened the sixth seal, and, lo, there was a great earthquake; and the sun became black as sackcloth of hair, and the moon became as blood;*
> *"And the stars of heaven fell unto the earth, even as a fig tree casteth her untimely figs, when she is shaken of a mighty wind.*
> *"And the heaven departed as a scroll when it is rolled together; and every mountain and island were moved out of their places."* [2]

---

[1] *Rev 6:9*

[2] *Rev 6:12-14*

CHAPTER SUMMARY

As one lists the events of the world as outlined in the Bible by the many different authors, you can see how much they are entwined one with another and how well they all fit and flow together. This is again a testimony of the spirit of prophecy as contained in the Holy Bible.

(Note: years/dates are approximate and only for general reference.)

1ST SEAL (4000 BC--3000 BC) [time of Adam]

2ND SEAL (3000 BC--2000 BC) [time of great wickedness/evil/violence]
(The Flood happened around 2300 BC, and Noah died around 2000 BC, 350 years after the flood.)

3RD SEAL (2000 BC--1000 BC) [time of great famines]
(Abraham and later Joseph in Egypt)

4TH SEAL (1000 BC--0 BC) [time of great famines/disease/wars]

*Head of the image	*Babylonia under Nebuchadnezzar	625--539 BC
*Breast/Arms of image	*Medes/Persia	539-331 BC
*Belly/Thighs of image	*Macedonia(Greece)	331–161 BC
*Legs of Iron of image	*Roman Empire	161 BC-- A.D.476+

5TH SEAL (0 AD--1000 AD) [time of great martydoms]

*Death of Christ	A.D. 33
*Apostles suffer great persecution & death	A.D.33-70
*Destruction of Jerusalem & temple	A.D. 70-73
*Jews scattered/captured "into all nations"	A.D. 73
*Jerusalem controlled by "Gentiles"	A.D. 70-- A.D.1967

(Starting of "times of Gentiles")

6TH SEAL (1000 AD--2000 AD)

*1st spiritual resurgence/reformation	1600
*Feet/Toes of image	*Holy Roman Empire/Early Europe 1800--

   *Kingdom of God (Daniel) comes forth   *2nd great spiritual
                          resurgence/ revival
                          1800--1860
  *Return of Jews to Israel/Jerusalem   1945-current
  *Jerusalem controlled by Jews   1967
   (Ending of *"times of Gentiles"*)

According to the chronology in Luke, it is after the Jews return to Israel and regain control of Jerusalem that the events of the last days really begin to happen. It is during *"this generation"* that all will be fulfilled and the Savior will come. Luke and Matthew record the following signs that will occur after the Jews regain control of Jerusalem:

  *Wars and rumors of war, nation against nation, kingdom against kingdom
  *Great earthquakes in divers places, famines, pestilences
  *Signs in the heavens
  *Seas & waves roaring
  *Men's hearts failing them
  *Great Earthquake
  *Sun darkened, Moon, Stars are darkened
  *Moon becomes as blood
  *Stars fall from heaven to earth
  *Great sign of Christ in Heavens

In his vision, it is the significant events of the very end of the 6th Seal that John begins to describe in more detail, adding some additional events as well. Some of these events he also describes in the very beginning or the "opening" of the 7th Seal since they are the events that signal the transition between the sixth and seventh Seals.

If we put Luke 21, Nebuchadnezzar's and Daniel's visions, along with Johns vision of the seven seals....the time line looks like this:

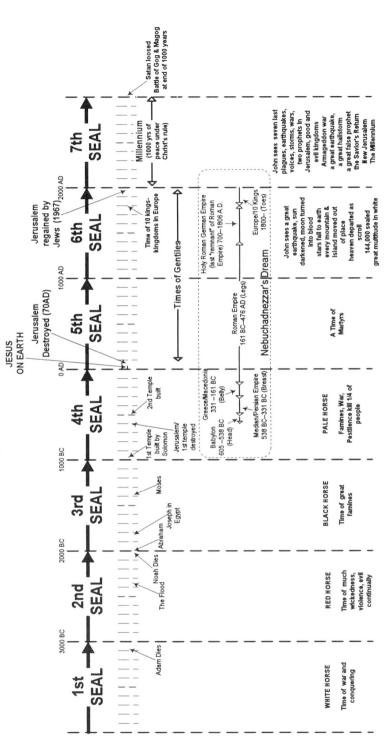

JOHN'S VISION OF EARTH'S EXISTENCE

JESUS ON EARTH

| 1st SEAL | 2nd SEAL | 3rd SEAL | 4th SEAL | 5th SEAL | 6th SEAL | 7th SEAL |

3000 BC · 2000 BC · 1000 BC · 0 AD · 1000 AD · 2000 AD

Satan loosed Battle of Gog & Magog at the end of 1000 years

Jerusalem regained by Jews (1967) 2000 AD

Jerusalem Destroyed (70AD)

Millennium (1000 yrs of peace under Christ's rule)

Time of 10 kings-kingdoms in Europe

— Times of Gentiles —

Adam Dies

Noah Dies — The Flood

Abraham — Joseph in Egypt

Moses

1st Temple built by Solomon

Jerusalem/ 1st temple destroyed

2nd Temple built

Jerusalem/ 1st temple destroyed

Nebuchadnezzar's Dream

Babylon 605–538 BC (Head)

Median/Persian Empire 538 BC–331 BC (Breast)

Greece/Macedonia 331–161 BC (Belly)

Roman Empire 161 BC–476 AD (Legs)

Holy Roman German Empire (last "remnant" of Roman Empire) 700–1806 A.D.

Europe/10 Kings 1800– (Toes)

WHITE HORSE
Time of war and conquering

RED HORSE
Time of much wickedness, violence, evil continually

BLACK HORSE
Time of great famines

PALE HORSE
Famines, War, Pestilence kill 1/4 of people

A Time of Martyrs

John sees a great earthquake, sun darkened, moon turned into blood stars fall to earth every mountain & island moved out of place heaven departed as scroll 144,000 sealed great multitude in white

John sees seven last plagues, earthquakes, voices, storms, wars, two prophets in Jerusalem, good and evil kingdoms Armageddon war a great earthquake, a great hailstorm a great false prophet the Savior's Return New Jerusalem The Millennium

And There Shall Be Signs

CHAPTER III
NATURE GONE WILD

Before we go any further in discussing the events of the last days as described in more detail by John the Revelator, it is important to understand that there are two general groupings of events or signs in the last days. First, there are those events that are very general and have very little specific information concerning them so that individual events are almost impossible to identify. Secondly, there are a group of events that have more detail concerning them so that it is possible to identify specific events or signs of the times.

GENERAL PLAGUES

As mentioned previously, in Luke and in Matthew, the Savior lists several of these general plagues, indicating that they would increase and become so great that Men's hearts would fail them for fear. Paul also describes some of these general plagues that would indicate the last days. Let us take a minute and discuss them briefly in relation to events that are happening around us.

> *"Then said he unto them, Nation shall rise against nation, and kingdom against kingdom:*
> *"And great earthquakes shall be in divers places, and famines, and pestilences; and fearful sights and great signs shall there be from heaven.*
> *"And there shall be signs in the sun, and in the moon, and in the stars; and upon the earth distress of nations, with perplexity; the sea and the waves roaring;*
> *"Men's hearts failing them for fear, and for looking after those things which are coming on the earth: for the powers of heaven shall be shaken."* [1]

WEATHER RELATED
(tempests, droughts, floods, famines, lightnings, thunderings)

All the time we hear the phrase about "abnormal weather" in that we are having "abnormal weather" around the world. (For example in Europe, July 1997, they had the worst flooding in 200 years. Already by May 1998, more people had died

---

[1]*Luke 21:10-11,25-26*

in the U.S. from tornados than in all of the previous year.) According to the scriptures, as we get closer to the Savior's coming, abnormal and extreme weather will actually be the norm from now on and will continue to get more severe and more extreme. Just pick up any newspaper and read about the weather. Droughts, floods, storms, hurricanes, tornados, freezes and other extreme weather in places and in seasons where they never were before are in almost every issue, producing famines that wipe out crops, animals, plant life and humanity. Spring comes earlier and is shorter. From the arctic to the antarctic, the weather in the world has gone haywire. El Nino comes and goes with devastating and disastrous results for the entire world. (The current drought in Brazil if continued could cause the death of 6 million people.) Truly the world's weather is "in commotion." One example, the lead paragraph in a recent article, is quoted below:

> "Glaciers are melting in the Alps and the Andes. Spring comes a week earlier in Canada where the forests are growing greener, but in the tropics corals are dying where the water is too warm. The world's temperature has gone up a degree since 1880, while severe rain and snowstorms have increased 20 percent in the United States."[1]

PESTILENCE/DISEASE

The scriptures also indicate that pestilences would be very prevalent the closer we get to the Savior's Coming. According to Luke, these should begin to increase significantly after 1967, or when the Jews regained control over Jerusalem. Indeed, we see that this has been the case. In the late '70s Aids burst upon the world. Since then it has geometrically increased it's terrible toll. In less than 20 years, AIDS/HIV infection had become the leading cause of death for the 25-44 year old male in the U.S[2]., and recent estimates (1998) indicate that there are currently 30 million people infected with HIV. Pfesteria, Hauntavirus, Ebola, Heart Disease[3], Cancer, Diabetes, Gonorrhea, Syphilis, Super Tuberculosis, Plague, Lyme disease, Gulf War Syndrom....are just a few of the diseases that are running rampant throughout the world. During these past twenty years, and particularly in the past ten years, the world has seen a veritable explosion of

---

[1] *Global Warming May Be Causing Wild Weather, Gannett News Service, May 18, 1997*

[2] National Center for Health Statistics, *1995 Report of Final Mortality Statistics, Vol.45 No.1(S2)*

[3] *In 1995 Heart disease was the leading cause of death in the U.S. with 839,000 deaths. Average life expectancy in the U.S. dropped in 1995. (Ibid)*

terrible diseases. Most have become incurable in that they are, or have become, immune to treatment by antibiotics. While many at one time where curable, most are now listed as fatal. Pestilences and new lethal diseases have become so prevalent in these last days that there are more and more books being written about the subject almost daily.

EARTHQUAKES

The U.S. Geological Survey reports that up until 1950 the number of killer quakes (6.0 or higher not including aftershocks) remained fairly constant, averaging between 2-4 per decade. In the 1950's there were nine. In the 1960's, there were 13. In the 1970's, there were 51. In the 1980's, there were 86. From 1990-1996 there have been more than 150, with 47 significant earthquakes in the world just in 1995. In 1996, the number almost doubled, increasing to 72. By March 5 of 1997 there had already occurred more deaths from earthquakes than in all of 1996. Currently, we are averaging approximately seven or more 6.0 earthquakes a month. Below is a graph charting this earthquake growth. Notice the trend?

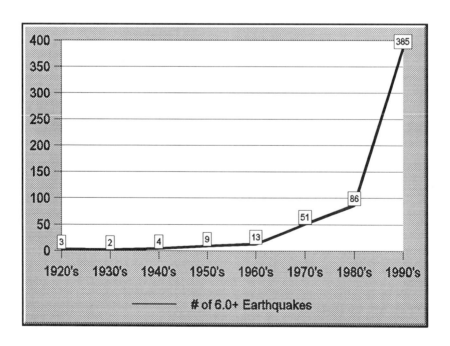

VOLCANOES

Interestingly enough, a very similar graph can be made by listing all of the major eruptions and new volcanoes that have appeared during the last 100 years.

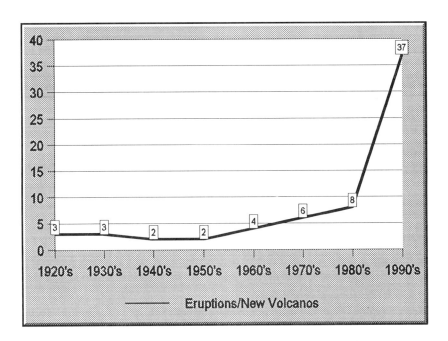

WARS & RUMORS OF WAR

Another graph like the ones above could be made for wars and other conflicts, which have steadily increased since the American Civil War, with a dramatic increase during the last 50 years. The United Nations reports that the violence/wars expected in 1998 will be almost double that in 1997. Anywhere one turns to in the world there is violence, war, rumors of war (terrorism?), happening on a daily basis.

SIGNS IN THE HEAVENS

The scriptures indicate that there would be signs in the heavens and on the earth, even to the point that the powers of heaven would be shaken.

> *"And there shall be signs in the sun, and in the moon, and in the stars; and upon the earth distress of nations, with perplexity; the sea and the waves roaring;*
> *"Men's hearts failing them for fear, and for looking after those things which are coming on the earth: for the powers of heaven shall be shaken."* [1]

In the past, God has used signs in the heavens to signify great events. Moses wrote that one of the reasons that the sun, moon and stars were placed in the heavens was for seasons and for signs.

> "And God said, Let there be lights in the firmament of the heaven to divide the day from the night; **and let them be for signs**, and for seasons, and for days, and years:
> "And let them be for lights in the firmament of the heaven to give light upon the earth: and it was so."[2]

Jesus's birth was heralded by special signs in the heavens, some of which only those who studied the stars and the heavens would recognize. (See Matt 2:1-10, the story of the 3 wise men who saw the star indicating the Savior's birth and knew where to go, while the wise men of Herod's court and all Jerusalem did not.)

To set the stage, here are some interesting happenings on some special days. The day(s) of Passover were declared by God to be a very special time and of extreme significance to the Jews. First, it must be understood that because the Jewish calendar is based upon the moon (it represents the Messiah in the heavens), and the Gregorian calendar is based upon the sun, therefore, the lunar day of Passover can fall anywhere between the Gregorian calendar dates of March 22 and April 25.

---

[1]*Luke 21:25-26*

[2]*Gen 1:14-15*

There is substantial evidence that Jesus was born on Passover (Thursday 6 April 1 BC), started his ministry on Passover (6 April A.D.30) and died three years later on Passover (April 1, 33 A.D.), exactly when the Paschal lamb was to be sacrificed. The Savior then arose from the grave on Sunday (the first day of the week), April 3, 33 A.D.

Passover 1996 (Thursday April 4)
The comet Hyakutake was at its closest approach to the earth on Passover 1996. The path that Hyakutake followed through the heavens at that time was between the handle of the big dipper, which, to the ancients, symbolized the flock of the good Shepherd, and Arcturus, meaning "he comes." The Book of Job (Job 38:32) refers to this group of heavenly bodies as "Arcturus with his sons" a good shepherd leading his flock.

Since the spring of 1996 there have been consecutive lunar eclipses on every major full moon feast day of Israel. The first occurred on Passover, the next on the Eve of the Feast of Tabernacles (Sept 27, 1996), and the third happened on Purim, March 3, 1997. Another fell in the middle of the Days of Repentance, September 16, 1997. The 1996-97 Jewish religious year will have begun and ended with lunar eclipses. It will be interesting to see what occurs during the next Jewish year and Passover.

Passover 1997 (Tuesday April 22)
The comet Hale-Bopp was also at its closest approach to the earth during Passover 1997. Hale-Bopp appeared from Sagittarius, "the double natured one" and continued through Opheuchus, "the Serpent Holder." It then journeyed across the constellation Orion. According to the Talmudic scholars, a comet crossing Orion signifies great tribulation for the earth.

Also, according to scientists, we are entering a period of increasing solar flare activity, which should peak in the year 2000[1] We are also expecting a great increase in meteorites coming into the earth's atmosphere and burning up. These are often referred to as "shooting stars" or "falling stars."

---

[1]*CNN SCI-TECH update, April 8, 1997*

Passover 1998 (Saturday April 11)
More of the same as in 1997, another less spectacular comet, "Stonehouse" was also at perihelion during Passover, increasing solar flare activity with intensities strong enough to disrupt communications and cause electronic damage, "falling stars" including the "Leonids" meteorite shower (this happens every 33 years and will peak around November 17th with perhaps as many as 100 meteroites per second. What should prove interesting is that the showers could disable many of the 500 satellites that are now orbiting the earth, something which hasn't been able to happen in the past.)

Passover 1999 (Thursday April 1)
Again, more of the same increased celestial activity, especially solar flare activity is being predicted by scientists. However, from September 1996 until Passover 1999 something very unusual will happen that only occurs every 11,000 years. The new moon (representing the Messiah according to the Talmud), will rise from the horizon directly in the constellation of Virgo and move within 24 hours to the feet of the "virgin," giving the impression that the "virgin" is giving birth to the moon or the "Messiah."

Passover 2000 (Thursday April 20)
Something else that will only occur every 11,000 years......starting just before Passover, April 20, 2000, and finally on May 7, 2000 (or Iyar 2, 2576 on the Hebrew calendar), Venus, Mercury, Jupiter, Saturn, Mars, the Moon and the Sun will appear from the earth to be lined up. According to Josephus, these seven bodies represent the menorah in the Temple (Antiquities 3. 11:7).

Also, May 7 is the traditional day that Solomon started building the First Temple and that Ezra started building the Second Temple. Will it be the time that the Jews start building the Third Temple?

Passover 2001 (Sunday April 8)
Another very rare occasion in that Passover coincides with Easter Sunday.

WICKEDNESS & SIN INCREASE

The Bible clearly states that one of the signs of the last days would be a great increase of wickedness and sin. One has only to look at any newspaper and see that integrity, morality, purity, and kindness has been replaced by dishonesty and deceit, rampant immorality (including the truly perverted sins of homosexuality and lesbianism. See Romans 1:18-32), darkness, evil and greed. Truly we are at the time that Isaiah spoke of when he said:

> *"Woe unto them that draw iniquity with cords of vanity, and sin as it were with a cart rope:*
> *"That say, Let him make speed, and hasten his work, that we may see it: and let the counsel of the Holy One of Israel draw nigh and come, that we may know it!*
> *"Woe unto them that call evil good, and good evil; that put darkness for light, and light for darkness; that put bitter for sweet, and sweet for bitter!*
> *"Woe unto them that are wise in their own eyes, and prudent in their own sight!*
> *"Woe unto them that are mighty to drink wine, and men of strength to mingle strong drink:*
> *"Which justify the wicked for reward, and take away the righteousness of the righteous from him!"* [1]

---

[1] *Isaiah 5:18-23*

CHAPTER IV

IDENTIFYING THE KINGDOM THAT EVENTUALLY GATHERS THE ARMIES TO ARMAGEDDON

TWO OPPOSING KINGDOMS IN THE LAST DAYS

Now that we have discussed some of the general plagues and events, let us continue on with John's description of more specific events, starting first with the description of two kingdoms, namely the kingdom of God that Daniel initially described as coming forth in the last days, and an evil kingdom coming forth to persecute and kill the righteous. If we can possibly identify either of these two kingdoms, and perhaps more importantly the beginning political kingdom that turns to evil and consumes the world, it will help us to possibly get an idea of how close we are to the Savior's coming.

In the Bible we read that in the last days just prior to the Second Coming of Jesus Christ, there would eventually emerge a great division of the people into two groups, or spiritual kingdoms, that represent the two eternal opposing forces, good and evil. Namely, they are the kingdom of God/Jesus and the kingdom of the Devil. Essentially, those *"which keep the commandments of God, and have the testimony of Jesus Christ,"*[1] or who take upon themselves the name of Christ and seek to keep His commandments are members of the kingdom of God. (There is no other way, because *Jesus is the only way*.) Those who reject or deny Jesus Christ and who do not seek to keep His commandments, essentially choosing to follow the teachings of Satan, make up the populace of the evil kingdom.

We read that the kingdom of God in the very last days, the much smaller of the two, continues to grow in numbers even though it is persecuted by the followers/members of the evil kingdom. In the end, just when things seem so hopeless and the evil kingdom is in complete control (very similar to just before the flood when *"the wickedness of man was great in the earth, and that every*

---

[1]*Rev 12:17*

imagination of the thoughts of his heart was only evil continually.[1]), the Savior calls forth those who have been striving to keep His commandments and then destroys the wicked. Those who have been members of the kingdom of God then return to the earth, inheriting it for a thousand years (called the Millennium) under the direct leadership of Jesus Christ.

Though the Bible talks of "kingdoms," it needs to be understood that these two kingdoms are essentially "spiritual" kingdoms and are not specifically political kingdoms though the evil one apparently starts out specifically as a political kingdom. Eventually, members of each kingdom will be of all nations, languages, races, etc. just like during the days of the early Apostles when the followers of Christ were a varied mixture of Jews, Romans, Greeks, Ethiopians, Cretians, etc., along with their opposition. It is the internal beliefs, desires and actions of individuals which denotes which kingdom they support and therefore belong to.

The key by which we can tell between the two kingdoms and their respective followers is found in the Savior's teaching, *"Wherefore by their fruits ye shall know them."* [2] Basically, Jesus taught His followers to serve God and to serve each other, even to do good to and bless their enemies.

> *"Jesus said unto him, Thou shalt love the Lord thy God with all thy heart, and with all thy soul, and with all thy mind.*
> *"This is the first and great commandment.*
> *"And the second is like unto it, Thou shalt love thy neighbour as thyself.*
> *"On these two commandments hang all the law and the prophets."* [3]

> *"For I was an hungered, and ye gave me meat: I was thirsty, and ye gave me drink: I was a stranger, and ye took me in: Naked, and ye clothed me: I was sick, and ye visited me: I was in prison, and ye came unto me...Verily I say unto you, Inasmuch as ye have done it unto one of the least of these my brethren, ye have done it unto me."* [4]

---

[1] *Genesis 6:5*

[2] *Matt 7:20*

[3] *Matt 22:37-40*

[4] *Matt 25:35-36,40*

Temperance, patience, godliness, brotherly kindness, humility,[1] honesty, personal integrity, purity, chastity, typify the followers of Christ. Whereas, hate, selfishness, a lying tongue, lust, force, pride, are those "fruits" that help identify the followers of Satan.

Another big difference is that Christ's doctrine is one of invitation and persuasion... never of force. Whereas, Satan's doctrine is to use whatever means will accomplish the spread of his doctrine... including lying and deceit, force of any kind, works of secrecy/darkness, murder, war and even genocide.

IDENTIFYING THE KINGDOM OF CHRIST IN THE LAST DAYS

As mentioned previously, Daniel, in his interpretation of the dream of Nebuchadnezzer, prophesied that there would be a succession of kingdoms leading up to a kingdom, or a group of political kingdoms, during which the spiritual kingdom of God would go forth, eventually becoming the kingdom which would be on the earth during the Millennium.

> *"And in the days of these kings shall the God of heaven set up a kingdom, which shall never be destroyed: and the kingdom shall not be left to other people, but it shall break in pieces and consume all these kingdoms, and it shall stand for ever.*
> *"Forasmuch as thou sawest that the stone was cut out of the mountain without hands, and that it brake in pieces the iron, the brass, the clay, the silver, and the gold; the great God hath made known to the king what shall come to pass hereafter: and the dream is certain, and the interpretation thereof sure. "*[2]

It would be after the time of the ten European nations, successors to the Roman Empire, that this kingdom of God would be established. More specific detail or information concerning this kingdom of God is not given clearly in the Bible. It is interesting to note that the flood of Christianity and revival in the gospel occurred in the 1500's--1800's, during the formation of modern Europe. In fact America was established and populated primarily with those who sought to live the gospel of Jesus Christ according to the dictates of their beliefs.

---

[1] *2 Peter 1:5-8, 1 Peter 5:5*

[2] *Daniel 2:44,45*

IDENTIFYING THE SPIRITUAL KINGDOM OF SATAN IN THE LAST DAYS

John the Beloved, in his Revelation, talks about this spiritual kingdom of God, even describing how its members are persecuted, even killed, because of their desire to serve Christ instead of the Devil. But additionally, he describes the ascendancy of this final spiritual kingdom of the Devil or Satan in the last days, going into some detail describing from what political kingdoms this Satanic kingdom comes forth in the last days, some of the more important actions of this evil kingdom, and how it persecutes the righteous while trying to destroy the kingdom of God.

John notes that this Satanic kingdom is very successful, to the point that just before the Savior comes, it controls all of the world, force-teaching and promulgating its evil anti-Christ doctrines over all the people of the earth except for a very few. John indicates that many of those who don't accept these doctrines and philosophies are murdered, and thus by lies and deceit, works of darkness, evil wealth, greed, murder and war, this evil kingdom corrupts all of the kingdoms of the earth, to the point that if the Savior does not come when He does, even the few righteous who are present would be destroyed.

The teachings of this evil kingdom are exactly opposite to those of Christ's kingdom and include such teachings as personal selfishness and aggrandizement, hate and bigotry towards others, rebellion against authority, lying/cheating and violence to get gain...in essence, the use of any means, including murder and war, to gain forceful dominion and power over others. Also, an important teaching is that there is no God, or that man is his own God, there is no devil either, hence, there is no such thing as good or bad except as each person defines it for himself. (Now called relativism and humanism.) The evil works of this kingdom are usually characterized by trying to be hidden from the eyes of men, by trying to perform them in "darkness."

Of course, Satan has also taught his "spiritual" tenets to the children of men throughout the existence of the earth. There are several occasions in the past where political kingdoms have been based upon these tenets. **In every instance when this has happened it has lead to the eventual destruction of such kingdoms and societies.** General Douglas McArthur wrote:

"History fails to record a single precedent in which nations subject to moral decay have not passed into political and economic decline. There has either been a spiritual awakening to overcome the moral lapse, or a progressive deterioration leading to ultimate national disaster."

The most notable example of this contained in the scriptures/history was when almost all of the world became *"evil continually"* during the time of Noah, apparently basing their society upon Satan's teachings. As a result, the Lord cleansed the earth from its wicked and evil inhabitants by a flood. (It is interesting to note that it is God who allows Satan to do this teaching of his evil "doctrines and philosophies" to the children of men, so that they might have the opportunity to choose between the two opposing philosophies and prove to themselves and the Lord their true characters. *"Choose you this day whom ye will serve,"*[1] is the cry of the Bible.)

Again, it is extremely important to note that a major difference between the two philosophies concerning political kingdoms is this... those kingdoms based upon or using Satan's philosophies/teachings almost always to try to overthrow, conquer and otherwise force their control and philosophies upon other kingdoms and peoples, while those kingdoms based upon or using Jesus Christ's philosophies desire to let other people/kingdoms choose for themselves and do not force their philosophies or control over anyone.

---

[1] *Joshua 24:15*

Identifying a Significant Political Kingdom of the Last Days

Even though the scriptures explain that in the last days all of the world, except a very few of the elect, would become evil and be a part of Satan's spiritual kingdom, there is a specific political kingdom of the world that the scriptures identify as the starting centerpiece to an eventual political kingdom based upon anti-Christ philosophies that comes to dominate the world just prior to the Savior's return. This kingdom embarks on a course that leads it to eventually oppose truth, persecute and kill the righteous, encourage wickedness and sin among its members, and helps to gather the armies of the world to the final battle at Armageddon. **(Basically, over a period of time, it adopts all of the tenets and philosophies of Satan's spiritual kingdom and comes to include all of the kingdoms of the world.)**

Listing the Political Kingdom's 19 Identifying Traits

There are approximately 19 different identifying references concerning this last evil kingdom and the kingdom or kingdoms that precede it. These are listed at the end of this chapter.

Let's begin and set the stage by starting in verse one of Revelation Chapter 13:

> *"And I stood upon the sand of the sea, and saw a beast rise up out of the sea, having seven heads and ten horns, and upon his horns ten crowns, and upon his heads the name of blasphemy."*

Again, this has pretty well been understood to mean another reference to Europe, the same that was identified by Daniel. After the fall of the Roman Empire the influence of the Holy Roman Catholic Church, referenced by the seven heads, was the solidifying basis for establishing the European kingdoms, originally called the Holy Roman German Empire.[1] The 10 crowns refer to the 10 major kingdoms

that eventually came from the Holy Roman Empire and made up the bulk of Europe.

---

[1] *The city of Rome was built upon seven hills.*

Revelation 13:2...describes how fierce this kingdom is and how Satan gives unto these ten kingdoms his power and great authority. A very terrible political kingdom.

> *"And the beast which I saw was like unto a leopard, and his feet were as the feet of a bear, and his mouth as the mouth of a lion: and the dragon gave him his power, and his seat, and great authority."*

Verse 3...is where it starts to specifically describe this kingdom.

> *"And I saw one of his heads [*one of the ten kingdoms*] as it were wounded to death; and his deadly wound was healed; and all the world wondered after the beast."*

Apparently one of the ten kingdoms of Europe is almost destroyed but comes back to life. This destruction or 'wound' came about as the result of war...verse 14 *"...which had the wound by a sword, and did live."* The question has always been asked... which European country did this have reference to? Several countries have been almost destroyed in one of the many wars that have been fought, and have made a come-back. France, Germany, Austria, Italy, Spain, etc. would all qualify to one degree or another.   Reading on in verse three, and following the life of this kingdom a little further, we find some more identifying features......the world worships this kingdom and the world is afraid to make war with it.

Verses 4-7...This kingdom speaks great things and blasphemies and has power to continue for 3½ years. This kingdom blasphemes God, makes war with the Saints and overcomes them, has power over all of the world and most of the world shall worship or support this kingdom, except those who are written in the book of life.

> *"And they worshipped the dragon which gave power unto the beast: and they worshipped the beast, saying, Who is like unto the beast? who is able to make war with him?*
> *"And there was given unto him a mouth speaking great things and blasphemies; and power was given unto him to continue forty and two months.*
> *"And he opened his mouth in blasphemy against God, to blaspheme his name, and his tabernacle, and them that dwell in heaven.*

> *"And it was given unto him to make war with the saints, and to*

overcome them: and power was given him over all kindreds, and tongues, and nations."

The Second Kingdom Comes To Power

Verses 11-14... Starting in these verses there is apparently another kingdom that comes to power. This second kingdom is actually two kingdoms, *"two horns,"* and speaks like Satan. *"Like a lamb"* would suggest that this second kingdom appears to be innocent or harmless at first. Later, this second kingdom gains all of the power of the first kingdom and causes the world to support or *"worship"* the first kingdom. This second kingdom also does great wonders and miracles which deceives those that dwell on earth, saying that the world should make an *"image"* to the first kingdom. It appears that somehow the two kingdoms are related or intertwined together.

> *"And I beheld another beast coming up out of the earth; and he had two horns like a lamb, and he spake as a dragon.*
> *"And he exerciseth all the power of the first beast before him, and causeth the earth and them which dwell therein to worship the first beast, whose deadly wound was healed.*
> *"And he doeth great wonders, so that he maketh fire come down from heaven on the earth in the sight of men,*
> *"And deceiveth them that dwell on the earth by the means of those miracles which he had power to do in the sight of the beast; saying to them that dwell on the earth, that they should make an image to the beast, which had the wound by a sword, and did live."*

Verse 15...In this verse, this second kingdom also has power to give life to the "image" of the first kingdom and causes those that do not support the "image" of the first kingdom to be killed. Put another way, the second kingdom has power to activate--*"give life unto"* the ideals and goals --*"image"* of the first kingdom and then causes all those who do not support these ideals/goals to be put to death.

> *"And he had power to give life unto the image of the beast, that the image of the beast should both speak, and cause that as many as would not worship the image of the beast should be killed."*

Verses 16-18... In these verses this second kingdom also causes everyone to receive a mark in their right hand or forehead. This mark is apparently a substitute for money or the authority to use money because "*no man can buy or sell, save he that had the mark, or the number.*" The number is 666 and apparently also refers to a man.

> "*And he causeth all, both small and great, rich and poor, free and bond, to receive a mark in their right hand, or in their foreheads:*
>
> "*And that no man might buy or sell, save he that had the mark, or the name of the beast, or the number of his name.*
>
> "*Here is wisdom, Let him that hath understanding count the number of the beast: for it is the number of a man; and his number is Six hundred threescore and six.*"

This is the end of Revelations, chapter 13. But this second kingdom is also mentioned in Revelations 15:2, and in 16:2,13-16. Accordingly, this second kingdom is joined by a false prophet, working miracles, and by these miracles gathers the world to Armageddon.

> "*And I say as it were a sea of glass mingled with fire: and them that had gotten the victory over the beast, and over his image, and over his mark, and over the number of his name, stand on the sea of glass, having the harps of God.*
>
> "*And the first went, and poured out his vial upon the earth; and there fell a noisome and grievous sore upon the men which had the mark of the beast, and upon them which worshipped his image.*
>
> "*...And I saw three unclean spirits like frogs come out of the mouth of the dragon, and out of the mouth of the beast, and out of the mouth of the false prophet.*
>
> "*For they are the spirits of devils, working miracles, which go forth unto the kings of the earth and of the whole world, to gather them to the battle of that great day of God Almighty.*
>
> "*Behold, I come as a thief. Blessed is he that watcheth, and keepeth his garments, lest he walk naked, and they see his shame.*
>
> "*And he gathered them together into a place called in the Hebrew tongue Armageddon.*"

Here, then, is a summary listing of these 19 identifying traits:

1. It is a country/kingdom of Europe.
2. This kingdom is all but destroyed by war and recovers.
3. The world wonders after this kingdom.
4. This kingdom speaks great things and blasphemies.
5. The world worships this kingdom.
6. The world is afraid to make war with this kingdom.
7. This kingdom has power to continue for 3 ½ years.
8. This kingdom blasphemes God.
9. This kingdom makes war against the saints and overcomes them.
10. This kingdom has power over all the earth.
11. A 2nd kingdom, made up of two kingdoms, appearing harmless at first, comes to power.
12. The 1st & 2nd kingdoms are somehow related. Possibly the 2nd kingdom is the successor to the first kingdom.
13. This second kingdom has all the power of the 1st kingdom or it also has power over all of the world.
14. This 2nd kingdom performs great wonders and miracles and deceives the world.
15. This 2nd kingdom gives life to the "ideals" of the 1st kingdom.
16. This 2nd kingdom kills all those that do not worship the ideals of the 1st kingdom.
17. This 2nd kingdom causes all of the world, except a few faithful, to receive a mark in order to buy or sell.
18. This 2nd kingdom is joined by a great false prophet, an anti-Christ, who performs miracles and deceives the world.
19. This kingdom and false prophet gathers an army to Armageddon.

Again we come to the question of, 'Which political country and its history fit these traits?'

NAMING A PARTICULAR POLITICAL COUNTRY

The key to the mystery is that the successor kingdom, or second kingdom is made up of actually two kingdoms or *"two horns."* Modern day events (interestingly enough, after 1967, or when the Jews regained Jerusalem) have suddenly provided a possible answer...the country that is now united that was made up of two countries is probably East and West Germany.[1] They are now united together again just like they were before World War II and before World War I. With this as a working hypothesis, we can now go back and see if the history of Germany fits the criteria of these first and second kingdoms.

Testing the Country For the 19 Identifying Traits

Traits 1 and 2.....Verses 1-3
1. It is a country/kingdom of Europe.
2. This kingdom is all but destroyed by war and recovers.

Of course, Germany has been and still is a major European country. From 900 A.D. to 1806 A.D. it was the center of the Holy Roman Empire, holding power over the remnants of the Roman Empire located in central Europe (which consisted primarily of the German States and was ruled by a long succession of German kings), which controlled and dominated the rest of Europe. This was called the First Reich.[2] During WWI and immediately after, Germany was almost totally destroyed and ruined. Of all of the countries involved in WWI, Germany

---

[1] *NOTE: Many have proposed that Communism will become or is the kingdom of the beast. They are correct in that Communism and socialism are part of the kingdom of the beast. However at this point in the prophecies, Communism alone does not fit all of the details mentioned above of the political kingdom specifically described as the "beast." However, Communism is definitely at the heart of the spiritual kingdom of Satan. Communism, Marxism, Naziism, Socialism are all just differing names for Satan's teachings. Satan's teachings will eventually gain spiritual control over Germany again, and eventually the entire world. But it is also just one of the many differing tools being used to subjugate the world to Satan's power. It is important to note that the controlling powers that behind the scenes helped cause the First World War and the Second World War by giving funds to first arm and then re-arm Germany were also the main agents that funded the establishment and rise of Communism in Russia and throughout the world. These international power brokers have helped to foment wars, revolution, confusion etc. in their quest for power. These powers, identified for many years as the powers that control the international banks, are on the verge of succeeding in their quest to overthrow or control the world. In actuality this is the seat or power of the Beast.*

[2] *"The territory of the empire originally included what is now Germany, Austria, Western Czechoslovakia, Switzerland, Eastern France, the Low Countries, and parts of Northern and Central Italy. But its sovereign was usually the German king, and the German lands were always its chief component; after the mid-15th century, it was known as the Holy Roman Empire of the German Nation....The German empire of 1871-1918 was often called the Second Reich (empire) to indicate its descent from the medieval empire; by the same reasoning, Adolf Hitler referred to Nazi Germany as the Third Reich."* The New Encyclopedia Britannica, *15th Edition, 1977, Volume V, p. 99*

was the worst off afterwards and almost disappeared as a country because of economic disaster, etc. as a result of the war and the forced war reparations. But Germany made a startling recovery. (It is interesting to note that this recovery, or "healing," of Germany was accomplished by Hitler in less than twenty years and was funded by the international banking community, under the direction of the Rothchilds.)

Traits 3, 5 and 6.....Verse 4
3. The world wonders after this kingdom.
5. The world worships this kingdom.
6. The world is afraid to make war with this kingdom.

Just prior to WWII, in the late 1930s, the world catered to Germany. Most of the world was starting to seek to be involved with the German Empire. Later, most of the world was involved heavily with Germany and the Nazi ideals. (Nazi was the abbreviated name given to National Socialism.) We are all familiar with the appeasement of Germany/Hitler before WWII. The phrases"who is like unto Germany" and "*Who is able to make war with him*" aptly reflect the attitude that was taken towards Germany and Hitler by most of the world.

Traits 4,7,8 and 10...Verses 5 & 6
4. This kingdom speaks great things and blasphemies.
7. This kingdom has power to continue for 3 ½ years.
8. This kingdom blasphemes God.
10. This kingdom has power over all the earth.

We are also very familiar with the great blasphemies or untruths that Hitler/Germany fostered upon the world. The Nazi ideals of racism, anti-semitism, elitism, hatred, the end justifying the use of any means, etc. have been well documented. Truly, the Nazis came to reflect the very teachings of Satan. There is no need to go into detail here.

Concerning the "*forty and two months*" or 3½ years, it is interesting to note that from the time that America declared war on Germany...December 8, 1941 (which truly made it a world war), to the time of the surrender of Germany on May 9,1945 was a period of almost exactly 3½ years.[1]

---

[1]*Added note: Late 1941 saw the main German armies push into Greece, push into Romania, push into Yugoslavia, push into Russia, and of course Japan, which had joined with Germany on September 27, 1940 forming the Axis powers,*
(continued...)

Trait 9....Verse 7
9. This kingdom makes war against the saints and overcomes them.

For anyone trying to serve Christ the war was very hard...especially in Europe. Those who tried to serve their fellow man, often by helping those who were being persecuted, were often destroyed. It was an extremely dark period for true Christians everywhere.

Traits 11 & 12...verse 11
11. A 2nd kingdom, made up of two kingdoms, comes to power.
12. The 1st & 2nd kingdoms are somehow related. Possibly the 2nd kingdom is the successor to the first kingdom.

Currently, as mentioned before, traits 11 and 12 have a unique fulfillment in recent history in the sudden and the surprising uniting of East and West Germany into a single country. In essence, Communism came from and was funded initially by Germany under Bismarck. [Again it is important to note that Fascism, Socialism and Communism have the same ideals, same goals (control over others), even generally the same techniques, but perhaps differing language and slightly different approaches. All end up being completely totalitarian regimes.] In essence the 2 horns not only represent the combining of East and West Germany, but the combining of Germany and Russia, or Fascism/Communism-Socialism together again to dominate the world. Just by uniting into a single Germany, United Germany has become one of the top three economic powerhouses in the world today, with the US and Japan being the other two. United Germany has been at the heart of several drastic and accelerated changes for its European neighbors, with the combining of all of Europe into a single "New World Power" it's goal. With the coming economic conversion to the Euro starting in 1999, United Germany-now becoming-United Europe may soon dominate the world. Even further, the United States and even the former countries of the East Communist Block, including Russia are in the process of adopting many of United Europe's laws and procedures, with the stated goal of becoming an integral part of this New World Order. It is interesting to note that the key, pivotal point to this one world government/global economy that the world is moving to, often called the New World Order, is the peaceful *"like a lamb"* joining of East and West

---

[1](...continued)
attacked Pearl Harbor as well as several other locations on December 7–10. All of this great initial expansion was accomplished/started in a matter of few months. Truly this period of time saw Germany really begin to dominate and exercise power over the world. .

Germany back into a single country.

RECAP
In a brief review then, for at least the first 12 identifying criteria of the first kingdom as described in Revelation Chapter 13, Germany and its history fits or fulfills them extremely well.

Testing the Country for Possible Future Fulfillment of Traits 13-19

How about the Rest of the Criteria Concerning this Second Kingdom, Does it Also Continue to Fit the Supposition of it Being United Germany?

The answer is yes ...and... probably. Since most of the criteria concerning this second kingdom of United Germany are events that happen in the future, except that it is two kingdoms combined into one kingdom, and that it is the successor to or aligned very closely to the first kingdom (identifying criteria #11 & #12), we would be speculating upon its possible fulfillment of prophecy...which is shaky ground at best. God often has unique and unforeseeable ways of fulfilling the prophetic word down to the last iota.

However, if the events ascribed to this second kingdom are close to fulfillment, which is the major point of this study, and we continue to work on the assumption that this second kingdom starts out as United Germany and then becomes controlled by world Communism/Fascism/Socialism (now called the New World Order), then we should be able to see at least the basis, or the beginning, of the potential fulfillment of these prophecies currently going on in Germany and Europe. Let us then proceed to look at whether or not we can see any of the beginnings to the possible fulfillment of prophecy concerning this second kingdom and the events of the last days. In Revelation 13:12-17, John describes some of the future actions of this second kingdom.

FUTURE TRAITS #13 & #15 & #16 and the Seeds For Their Potential Fulfillment

Verse 12...United Germany comes to power and begins to control and dominate the world again as before, and will cause the world to "*worship*" the old Germany.

I believe "_worship_" means that United Germany, because of its strength and power, causes the world to glorify and generally follow after the old German ideals and power (represented throughout the world today as the humanistic teachings/dogma of the New World Order), much like the world did in Bismarck's time and Hitler's time. For example, as one studies the writings, pronouncements, philosophies and even the language of Nazi Germany and its methods of rising to power, the similarities between Naziism then, and the New World Order now, are almost identical. Anti-Christian/anti-God and anti-family teachings, the removal of religion as an influence in society, suppression of individual rights, a disregard of human life (euthanasia concepts), anti-morality teachings (the concept that there is no real right or wrong or that right and wrong are relative concepts or that the government can define morality instead of God), selected racism, are all 1930's Nazi teachings. All power came to be centered in the government with the emphasis placed on group ideals and benefits, as determined by the government. These teachings and concepts were brought about through government interdiction and takeover (nationalization) of the education system, health/medical industry and almost all aspects of German life. By the early 1940's, the Nazi German government controlled almost all aspects of a German citizens life, in essence supplanting God and religion as the most important aspect of such a life. In the historical takeovers of socialism/communism of countries, the almost exact same procedures have been used as well.

Beyond the well-documented economic and political influences that Germany is beginning to exercise, if Germany is the 2nd kingdom and the time of its fulfillment of prophecy is very close, then there should be additional evidences that the past "ideals" or attitudes are returning as well.

One of the most important false ideas from prior Germany was something termed "super nationalism," or the idea that Germany was the greatest world power and its people the greatest people and that it should control/dominate or rule the world. This was the general basis of the first, second and third Reichs. Hitler carried this concept to the races as well...i.e. that the German race "the Aryans" were the master race. This was carried out even to the extreme point of eliminating the trash/unworthy races, which Hitler identified primarily as the Jews but was extended to any group that opposed him. The Germans, and their sympathizers, blamed the Jews as the cause of everything that was wrong and evil in the world and so deserved to be destroyed.

ARE WE SEEING A REVIVAL OF THIS OLD "ATTITUDE OF RACIAL HATE/BIGOTRY" AND NATIONALISM CURRENTLY?

A trip to the library, searching through newspapers and newsmagazines, surprisingly brings out the point that, yes, unfortunately, this concept of national bigotry, racism and anti-Semitism is on an extremely sharp rise all over the world, but especially in Europe, Germany and Russia (the area of the "beast"). The anti-Jewish movement in France, for example, now controls over 30% of the vote/population in some areas and is becoming a major factor in French politics. Racial and ethnic attacks in Germany, France, and other European countries are steadily increasing. Ethnic cleansing was, and still is, the root cause for the genocidal violence happening in the Balkans.

In Russia, there is violence against the Jews again...even pogroms. This has increased so much during the last few years that Israel declared that because of this surge in violence and the danger of even more excessive violence in Russia against the Jews, Russian Jews may travel and immigrate to Israel on the Jewish Sabbath. Many have been the articles concerning the rise of the United Germany, the rise of Nationalism, and the fears of these things leading to bringing about a Fourth German Reich.

Future Trait #14....Fire From Heaven
Verse 13....maybe this could have reference to nuclear weapons, of which Germany and other surrounding countries have a plentiful supply.

Future Traits #14 & 18....A Future False Prophet
Verse 14...In Rev 16:13-14 it says that this kingdom is joined by a great false prophet, who by means of miracles shall deceive the world and almost deceives the elect of God. (See Rev 19:20) The emergence of this false prophet/Anti-Christ is one of the very last events prior to the Savior's coming. At this stage in time, such a prophet or great religious leader has not emerged, though there are several potential candidates. (This is discussed later.)

Verse 15...Again, "image," meaning the ideals/concepts of Old Germany, will come forth very similar to the days prior to WWII. Again, there is evidence that this is beginning to happen as discussed above.

Future Trait #17...A World Monetary System

Verses 16-17...This appears to be one of the most important future events ascribed to this second kingdom. It is mentioned in Rev 14:9, and again in 15:2 as the major stumbling block for the *"saints"* to overcome in the last days in order to keep the commandments and faith of Christ. The event is that this second kingdom somehow causes all of the world to join in a world monetary system that it controls. No one is able to buy or sell unless he has joined this system, worshiped the ideals of this kingdom, and received its mark. All those who oppose this system are killed.

A world monetary system has been talked about for years but nothing has really moved towards it until the two Germanys became united. Now, things have changed and are continuing to change at an almost unbelievable rate. Europe is in the process of becoming a single economic unit and is switching over to a single currency, the Euro, starting in 1999.

GATT (in 1992), NAFTA (1993) and other treaties signed by the United States, Canada and Mexico are steps toward a similar economic goal for all of North America. In the New World Order envisioned and promoted by the United Nations and the global elitists, the long term plans call for four major regional economic zones, under the control of global committees set up by the United Nations. The plan requires the United States and other countries to give up their individual sovereign control/decision making to a central governing group such as those being set up in Europe. For the citizens of the United States, this is a two step process. First the government needs to gain control over an area by passing laws regulating it. Then this control is passed onto an "international" agency or committee. This is being accomplished slowly, but steadily.

Current U.S. governmental policy is to move towards a state where the government controls everything, increasingly similar to Nazi Germany and many communistic/socialistic states. Interestingly enough, much of the proposed Clinton agenda is an almost exact duplicate of old Nazi Germany legislation prior to WWII. The Gatt treaty and other similar proposals are direct economic moves towards this New World Order.

The "mark" of the beast could be a reference to something physical or to something spiritual, or to both. Spiritually, the mark of the beast could refer to those individuals who have given themselves over to the power and influence of

Satan and have been sealed his, just as the righteous who give themselves to obedience to the commandments of the Lord are sealed to the Lord.

Concerning a possible physical explanation of the "mark" in their right hands or foreheads that everyone must have in order to "buy or sell", we are very rapidly approaching the goal of becoming a true "cashless society". It is very common, almost a necessity, to get a credit card that can be used at almost any and every store, from fast food to grocery stores, which automatically can debit or transfer funds directly from an account, allows a person to pick up cash at any ATM across the world and allows one to even automatically initiate a loan if they so desired.

In a recent feature article, *The Future of Money* (April 27, 1998), Time magazine discussed how the world economy is in the process of changing into a single global, cashless, digital economy controlled by computers. It describes how a single computer chip will be the equivalent of cash, credit cards, ATM cards, checks, insurance policies, drivers license, social security, medical history, etc. and how this chip will soon be implanted under the skin of citizens worldwide.

This micro-chip, a little larger than a grain of rice, is now required to be implanted in animals in several parts of the country as a means of licensing and controlling them instead of the use of animal tags, and is even being used for human monitoring on many military bases.

Verse 18...The number of the mark of this 2nd kingdom has something to do with the number 666. One potential explanation of this is that the Universal Bar Code that appears on almost all packaging for sale has different bars of lines, or bar codes, in different combinations that represent the assigned number of the item. If you look at the bar code, you will find that there are usually two thin bars/lines together that start at the beginning, come in the middle and also signal the end of the number. If you look on the old universal bar code definition code sheet those lines represent the number six. And so in essence you have the number 666 in every universal bar code. In order to keep track of the hundreds of millions of products using bar codes all over the world, a huge computer complex was built. It is this computer which issues or assigns all of the universal bar codes in the world through it's sub-offices located in different countries. Again, interestingly enough, this computer complex is located in Belgium, which in the past was considered a part of Germany. The new global standard for this universal bar code is called the EAN and is being issued from the same area.

Another potential explanation of the number 666 is that the true way that it was meant to be used or understood was not passed on in the translation from the original Greek.

Briefly, in Greek and in Hebrew many of the letters of the Alphabet have corresponding number values. For example, the Greek letter Alpha, is the numerical equivalent of one or the first. Beta=2, stigma=6, xi=60, chi=600 and so forth. Therefore, any word or name in Greek could have a numerical equivalent by adding all of the corresponding values of each letter in the name. In Greek this practice is called Isopsephia and in Hebrew it is called Gematria. In essence, it was pretty much a one way code and only those who were privy to the original "key," or what the original word was, would know what the numerical equivalent stood for. Interestingly, in identifying this evil kingdom of the last days, John says: *"Let him that hath understanding count the number of the beast;"* and then perhaps as a further clue he adds, *"for it is the number of a man."* Or perhaps, in other words let those who are in the know add up the value of the name of the kingdom/beast, it is the same number as a man and the value of the letters are six hundred and sixty six. The Greek letters used for 666 are "chi, xi, stigma." The question then is the number 666 possibly a Gematria, or number code, that adds up to the value of 666 instead of a literal translation?

A clue was perhaps given by Irenaeus, Bishop of Lyons, who lived in the 2nd century, in that he wrote in his work, *AGAINST HERESIES*, a section devoted to trying to unravel the Gematria that was used in John's use of 666. Overall, though only removed less than 100 years from John's writing of Revelation, Iranaeus admits that many names are capable of yielding the number 666 and concludes

that he really doesn't know who or what kingdom John is referring to.[1]   In essence, perhaps we need to be careful about attributing too much to the importance of the number 666 in identifying the kingdom/beast.

However, even considering all of the above, it is extremely interesting to note that the definition for the Greek letter stigma (6) is "A mark pricked in or branded upon the body. In ancient oriental usage, slaves and soldiers bore the name or the stamp of their master or commander branded or cut into their bodies to indicate what master or general they belonged to, and there were even some devotees who

---

[1] (For more information see *SIX HUNDRED SIXTY-SIX BUT NOT 666* by Edward L. Pothier, July 1991 at www.math.gatch.edu/~jkatz/Religions/ Numerics/six.html.)

stamped themselves in this way with the token of their gods."

Future Trait #19...Gathering the Armies to Armageddon

By the time that this happens, the kingdom of the "Beast" is no longer just Germany, or even just Europe. By this time, most of the world belongs to this political and spiritual kingdom of Satan. In essence, there will only be two groups of people....those people who by their actions support this kingdom versus a much, much smaller group that has been ostracized from the mainstream world because they refuse to participate in the wicked and evil practices of a degenerate world. The Holy Bible mentions several countries and areas by name that are involved as the core groups in the battle of Armageddon. (See map on page 72)   It is important to note that of all these specifically mentioned countries, currently we see them coming together into two groups, United Europe and countries being involved in the militant Islamic fundamentalist movement. This will be discussed in more detail at a later time.

ADDITIONAL SCRIPTURAL CONFIRMATION

In Daniel's first vision, recorded in Daniel Chapter Seven, he has a vision of four beasts or kingdoms that come forth.   The fourth beast/kingdom is also described as having ten horns, which brings to mind the ten horned beast that John described. If they are describing the same kingdom or events, does the description of this kingdom and its subsequent kingdoms as recorded in Daniel fit the scenario just outlined?   Luckily, Daniel asks for an interpretation of the fourth kingdom since it is so terrible and "*shall devour the whole earth.*"

This fourth kingdom does the following things:
1. This fourth kingdom is terrible and strong and stamps to pieces all other kingdoms and controls the world.
2. Out of this kingdom would arise ten other kingdoms
3. Out of these ten kingdoms would arise another kingdom, diverse from the first, which would subdue three of the other ten kingdoms.   This kingdom was "*more stout than his fellows.*"
4. This kingdom shall speak great words against God.
5. Shall wear out the saints of the Most High and think to change times and laws.
6. This kingdom shall make war and have power over the saints for "*a time*

and times and the dividing of time."

7. Eventually this kingdom shall be judged and destroyed, while the other ten kingdoms appear to last a little longer.

"I beheld even till the beast was slain, and his body destroyed, and given to the burning flame.

"As concerning the rest of the beasts, they had their dominion taken away: yet their lives were prolonged for a season and time."[1]

Again, if we theorize that the fourth kingdom that rules the world was the Roman Empire, then from the Roman Empire we have the ten kingdoms that form the basis of Europe. Germany, obviously more stout or stronger than any other European nation, rises from the ten kingdoms and subdues three others (Bavaria, Prussia, and Austria could be those three). If "*time*" is interpreted as one year, then the time Daniel mentions would equal 3 ½ years [*a time* (1 year)*times* (2 years) *and the dividing of time* (1/2 year)], which fits the description of Germany during the war the same as in John's account. Warring against the saints or the righteous, speaking great things and great words against God, and thinking to change times and laws also could very easily apply to Germany as mentioned previously and similarly by John.

Again, Germany, as this very last kingdom described by Daniel, seems to fit extremely well in all of the particulars.

---

[1]*Daniel 7:11-12*

RECAP.....

The answer to the question "Can we see any of the beginnings to the possible fulfillment of future prophecy concerning this second kingdom in United Germany and world events?....is a surprisingly strong "yes".

The rise of this kingdom from Europe is another sign that we are at the very end of the Sixth Seal, because it seems to be something that starts in the Sixth Seal and yet is specifically mentioned after the opening of the Seventh Seal. Again, there appears to be a few events that are right in the middle of the crossover between the Sixth Seal and the very beginning of the Seventh Seal.

CHAPTER V

THE SEVEN LAST PLAGUES OF THE WRATH OF GOD

There are additional scriptures that continue to shed light on the future events concerning the Second Coming of the Lord. The rise of this second kingdom or New World Order, is just a part of the many events that are transpiring at this time, though it is an extremely important part. The events described in Revelation Chapter Thirteen describe only a portion of the events that will happen as the time of the Lords coming approaches. It details some of the main political conspiracies that will take place. In other places John describes some of the more "physical" events that are to take place such as natural phenomenon (unnatural weather, storms, earthquakes, etc.), as well as wars.

Over View Discussion

In Revelations 8, 9, 10 & 11, John describes seven angels, each with a trumpet and a plague that is released upon the earth. These are divided up into two categories, the first four and the last three, which are also called the three "Woes." As the plagues progress, or as they describe events closer to the Savior's coming, they generally get more specific in detail and description. There is another reference to seven plagues in Chapters 15 and 16 of Revelation as well, and are called the *"seven last plagues...of the wrath of God."* These seven plagues are extremely similar to the seven plagues mentioned in Revelations Chapter 8-11 with just a few differences. It appears that both of these references generally describe the same events, sometimes bringing out or describing different aspects of these last seven plagues.[1]

---

[1] *The reasoning is thus. Both sets of plagues are made up of seven plagues which occur after the seventh seal is opened, and the fact that in both sets of plagues, plague #2 in each refers to things dying in the sea, and in plague #3 both sets again refer to "rivers and fountains of waters", in plague #4 both refer to the "sun" and its involvement in the plague, and the fact that plague #6 in both sets involve or describe the army of Armageddon, finally and most importantly both sets of plagues have for their seventh plague the unveiling of the temple of the Lord in heaven, which very definitely describes the same event. The only real differences between the two accounts is found in the first plague in which both versions describe apparently different things, and in the chapter eight account of the plague of the sea, 1/3 of the sea*

(continued...)

Though the Lord has not given us the exact time of His coming, He has provided us many important details and signs which he has commanded the faithful to watch for, in order that they might be forewarned, and therefore prepared for the events as they unfold.

Jesus said in Luke that it would be after the Jews return and regain control of Jerusalem that the events of the last days would begin in earnest, and so we can infer that they will probably start in earnest after 1967. Again, it is important to understand that for the most part no other time references are given for the fulfillment of the "plagues" except for the last three...#5, #6, and #7. In other words, how long it takes for the first four plagues to come forth and be fully fulfilled is not given. Some plagues might be fulfilled in days, others in months, and yet others over years. One plague may start while a previous plague is in the process of fulfillment. Another point is that those things necessary to bring about the plague may have begun, and therefore the plague has started but it may be several years before the plague is in fulfillment enough for it to be observed or noticed by us. However all of the plagues, no matter when they started or how long it takes for them to be finished, will be completely fulfilled when the Savior makes his appearance to the world.

Additionally it is important to understand that, just as it was in the days of Moses in Egypt (as the plagues came forth life in Egypt tried to go on, coping day by day with the events as they were happening), so it will be for the people in the last days. We are told that even up to the last plague, almost to the very minute that the Savior comes, the world in general will be "*eating and drinking, marrying and giving in marriage,*" trying to cope with, explain away, and generally ignore the events happening around them.

It is important to realize that though Germany, at the beginning, may form the heart of the political kingdom called the "beast" in the scriptures, before long **this political kingdom includes most of the countries of the world, and eventually all of the kingdoms of the world become a part of it.** Spiritually speaking, the

---

[1](...continued)
creatures died along with 1/3 part of the ships, while in the chapter 16 account "every living soul died in the sea." Perhaps this plague starts with 1/3 of the sea life dying and then later some catastrophic event (such as a large meteor hitting the ocean) destroys the ships and all of the life in the sea.

kingdom of the "beast" is anyone or any group of people who oppose truth, seek to subjugate others, commit murder and violence, and adhere to or condone wicked or immoral practices as defined by the Lord.

LAST PLAGUE #1

> ***Rev 16:2..*** *"And the first went, and poured out his vial upon the earth; and there fell a noisome and grievous sore upon the men which had the mark of the beast, and upon them which worshipped his image."*

> ***Rev 8:7*** *"The first angel sounded, and there followed hail and fire mingled with blood, and they were cast upon the earth: and the third part of trees was burnt up, and all green grass was burnt up.*

The bible also translates "noisome" as bad or evil. Apparently some sort of evil plague attacks those who have the physical mark, as well as those who have the spiritual mark, of Satan. (Such an evil spiritual mark is placed upon those who serve Satan, just as a good spiritual mark is placed upon the righteous who serve Jesus. See Rev 7:3, 22:4.... 13:16; 14:9-11; 20:4)

Could this event be a reference to a particular devastating world-wide plague such as Aids? It is interesting to note that for those individuals that keep Christ's commandments concerning chastity, the odds of getting the HIV virus or AIDS are better than 500,000 to one in the U.S.. Simply put, "faithful, monogamous couples are not at risk." While among Gay men and women who are involved in wicked and immoral practices according to the Lord[1] the odds are better than 2 to 1, and intravenous drug users are quickly approaching the same level.

During the same time as this plague against wicked men begins, the destruction by fire of 1/3 of the trees and all of the grass also begins. This could very accurately be describing the deforestation that is happening all over the world, mostly by burning. All over the world during the past several years, including the U.S., the destruction of forests, primarily by burning, has been well documented.

---

[1] *The practice of Homosexuality has long been denounced as a selfishly evil, immoral and wicked practice by the Lord and His prophets. See Lev. 18:22, Deut. 23:17, Rom. 1:27, 1 Cor. 6:9*

Such destruction is almost a weekly article in the news. Austrailia, Brazil, South America, Mexico, Guatemala, Honduras, Nicaragua, Indonesia, Alaska, and many other places are all on fire burning out of control. However, the major destruction of 1/3 of the trees and grass could take place during the catastrophic events later described by John, such as during the major wars.

LAST PLAGUE #2

> ***Rev 8:8-9***..."*And the second angel sounded, and as it were a great mountain burning with fire was cast into the sea: and the third part of the sea became blood; And the third part of the creatures which were in the sea, and had life, died; and the third part of the ships were destroyed.*"

> ***Rev 16:3***... "*And the second angel poured out his vial upon the sea; and it became as the blood of a dead man: and every living soul died in the sea.*"

This staggers the imagination. Both references describe the plague as it affects the sea. What is John trying to describe with the words "*...as it were a great mountain burning with fire was cast into the sea....*"? Some type of cataclysmic event, a volcano exploding like Krakatoa did many years ago[1], or perhaps a huge falling meteor. Both types of events, if large enough, would create huge tidal waves that could cause 1/3 of the ships to be destroyed, all men on the sea to die and a third of all sea creatures to die. The Bible also gives some evidence that during a tremendous earth-shattering earthquake (the second "woe"), the islands and perhaps even the continents will be moved and brought back together as perhaps they were in the days before Peleg. The sea becoming blood and life dying could also be a reference to the terrible polluting of the sea, which is currently taking place, and would be expected from the terrible wars that have been prophesied for the future.

---

[1]*Krakatoa erupted in August, 1883. The resulting tidal wave killed over 35,000 people.*

LAST PLAGUE #3

Rev 16:4... "And the third angel poured out his vial upon the rivers and fountains of waters; and they became blood."

Rev 8:10-11..." And the third angel sounded, and there fell a great star from heaven, burning as it were a lamp, and it fell upon the third part of the rivers, and upon the fountains of waters; And the name of the star is called Wormwood: and the third part of the waters became wormwood; and many men died of the waters, because they were made bitter."

This prophecy is unique because it is associated with a name...*Wormwood*. Here John describes what appears to be a meteor that falls from heaven and causes a poisoning of the fresh waters upon the earth, or perhaps he is searching for words to try and describe something more modern such as the terrific meltdown of a nuclear power plant or even a nuclear bomb. A meltdown, or meltdowns, that spreads atomic dust and debris over 1/3 of the fresh waters of the earth is not too far fetched. The Chernobyl nuclear power plant meltdown in Russia (April, 1986) is a perfect example of such a catastrophe, the devastating effects of which we still are learning about and which many believe are far worse than at first indicated by scientists.[1] Atomic debris was spread over a large portion of Russia and over most of Europe, contaminating the water, land and vegetation. Ionizing radiation increased in the United States as well. This lead some experts to declare that an unexplainable jump in the death rate in the U.S. of over 40,000 deaths immediately following the accident, was probably caused indirectly by the accident, in addition to the thousands who died as a direct result. Interestingly enough the English translation of the Ukranian name Chernobyl is wormwood (a very bitter plant that grows wild in the region[2]), a coincidence more than remarkable.[3]

---

[1] *Note: Since this was written in 1989, much more has been revealed concerning the disaster of Chernobyl. It was far worse than was at first revealed. The meltdown itself reached the groundwater, contaminating the underground river that flows through the area. Officials now believe that as much as 1/3 of the freshwater in Russia has been contaminated. Dairy herds in England still produce milk laden with radiation poisoning. The death toll continues to rise. Unfortunately, currently there are 2 more reactors being operated at Chernobyl, of the same type and with the same problems as the first reactor. They have been described as future meltdowns waiting to happen.*

[2] *Wormwood in Ukrainian is Chornobyl (Chernobyl), the name for a marshy area near Kiev or Kyiv. The bitter taste of wormwood comes from absinthin and anabsinthin. Another constituent is thujone, an oil known to cause convulsions in rats in relatively low concentrations. One half ounce of wormwood oil caused convulsions and unconsciousness in a human foolish enough to tempt it. Long term use builds up*

(continued...)

LAST PLAGUE #4

> ***Rev 16:8-9***... *"And the forth angel poured out his vial upon the sun; and power was given unto him to scorch men with fire. And men were scorched with great heat, and blasphemed the name of God, which hath power over these plagues: and they repented not to give him glory."*

> ***Rev 8:12***...*"And the forth angel sounded, and the third part of the sun was smitten, and the third part of the moon, and the third part of the stars; so as the third part of them was darkened, and the day shone not for a third part of it, and the night likewise."*

This very easily could describe something that many of the world's scientists finally believe is happening, which is the global warming of the earth's atmosphere. (However, the debate is starting to center on what the cause of the global warming is.) We are told that an increase of just a few degrees would wreak havoc to the earth's climates. Computer projections concerning the U.S. indicate that such warming would cause the weather to be really abnormal in that bad or extreme weather would increase, or that there would not be such a thing as "normal" weather again. For example, it would flood where normally it didn't, it would cause an increase of tornadoes even in places that normally didn't have them, droughts and unusually hard freezes would occur, etc. Additionally, because of the worsening atmosphere, the sun is in a way "hotter" to mankind, in that, because of the increased ultra-violet rays of the sun actually striking the earth, there has been a noticeable increase in skin cancer. With great pollutions, smoke, disappearance of the protective ozone layer and other things happening, an increase in the global temperatures would be accelerated even more. There are additional Biblical references that the sun, moon and stars become darkened because of the effects of a tremendous future war. (See Joel 2:1-10)

---

[2]*(...continued)*
toxic effects. Internal or culinary use is strongly discouraged, especially long-term. Extract of wormwood containing absinthe is found in a few European alcoholic beverages (notably Strega), but due to health hazards from internal ingestion of absinthe, this use is fading fast. A turn of the century potent alcoholic drink called Absinthe was popular in Paris; frequent users were strongly prone to violent or self-destructive behavior well beyond that seen with plain alcohol. Today, very small amounts may be found in vermouth, as a flavoring which goes a long way.

[3] *See Chernobyl Fallout, S. Shulman, Technology Review 92:12-13 F/March 1989*

Now we come to the first of the three "woes" wherein John adds a lot more detail in his descriptions, enough detail so that the when these singular events happen, there would be very little question concerning them.

LAST PLAGUE #5: A STRANGE WAR...*THE FIRST "WOE"*

Rev 16:10-11... *"And the fifth angel poured out his vial upon the seat of the beast; and his kingdom was full of darkness; and they gnawed their tongues for pain, And blasphemed the God of heaven because of their pains and their sores, and repented not of their deeds."*

Rev 9:1-12... *"And the fifth angel sounded, and I saw a star fall from heaven unto the earth: and to him was given the key of the bottomless pit.*

"And he opened the bottomless pit; and there arose **asmoke out of the pit, as the smoke of a great furnace; and the sun and the air were darkened by reason of the smoke of the pit.**

"And there came out of the smoke locusts upon the earth: and unto them was given power, as the scorpions of the earth have power.

"And it was commanded them that they **should not hurt the grass of the earth, neither any green thing, neither any tree***; but only those men which have not the seal of God in their foreheads.*

" And to them it was given that they **should not kill them***, but that they* **should be tormented five months***: and their torment was as the torment of a scorpion, when he striketh a man.*

"And in those days **shall men seek death, and shall not find it; and shall desire to die, and death shall flee from them.**

"And the shapes of the locusts were like unto horses prepared unto battle; and on their heads were as it were crowns like gold, and their faces were as the faces of men.

"And they had hair as the hair of women, and their teeth were as the teeth of lions.

"And they had breastplates, as it were breastplates of iron; and the sound of their wings was as the sound of chariots of many horses running to battle.

> *"And they had tails like unto scorpions, and there were stings in their tails: and **their power was to hurt man five months**.*
>
> *"And they had a king over them, which is the angel of the bottomless pit, whose name in the Hebrew tongue is Abaddon, but in the Greek tongue hath his name Apollyon.*
>
> *"One woe is past; and, behold there come two woes more hereafter."*

Many times the Lord uses the term "darkness" to describe evil or wicked things. In the description of this plague it is used to describe the evil and wickedness that is a part of Satan's kingdom, and where there is evil and wickedness in great measure there is always violence and usually war. Plague #5 very definitely describes a particular war that has some peculiarities to it that set it apart from all other wars. This war is further labeled as the first of three terrible final "woes." **While all previous plagues do not have any specific time frame for completion mentioned, this plague does.** Also its completion, or fulfillment signals that the Savior's return is very rapidly approaching.

There are six things that are mentioned in this passage of scripture that set this war apart as extremely strange. They are: 1.) Smoke, 2.) Modern Mechanized Armies, 3.) Power for five months, 4.) Nothing green is hurt, 5.) This army does not kill many men, and 6.)Men will want to die, but death will flee them... John indeed describes some very peculiar things associated with this war. No war prior to 1967 would fit these six identifiers (especially the detail which states that nothing green is hurt), but interestingly enough, all of these strange "descriptions" find remarkable fulfillment in a fairly recent event in the Middle-East known more commonly as the Gulf War.

1. Smoke that darkens the sun and air would certainly describe the smoke from all of the burning oil wells from the war in Iraq/Kuwait. At no other time, that we are aware of, has there been such a pollution of the air. Interestingly enough, it was often described as "apocalyptic".

2. Modern Mechanized Armies. Of course the armies involved, over 1,000,000 men plus their equipment, could be described here. Interesting to note that the warfare consisted of primarily tanks, planes and helicopters with almost no men fighting hand to hand, which would give good reason why the Apostle John did not mention men in his account. Verses 7-10 very easily could be John's way of trying to describe this modern day war equipment:

> *"And the shapes of the locusts were like unto horses prepared unto battle; and on their heads were as it were crowns like gold, and their faces were as the faces of men. And they had hair as the hair of women, and their teeth were as the teeth of lions. And they had breastplates, as it were breastplates of iron; and the sound of their wings was as the sound of chariots of many horses running to battle. And they had tails like unto scorpions, and there were stings in their tails:"*

3. Power for five months. From the day that Iraq's armies crossed into Kuwait until the offensive began to drive them out of Kuwait, the time was approximately five months.

4. Nothing green is hurt. The Iraq/Kuwait war took place in one of the most desolate areas on the earth. Nothing but sand and rocks. Trees or grass weren't even available to be destroyed.

5. This army apparently does not do a lot of killing or cause a lot of deaths like the 6th plague army that kills a third part of men. Instead, this army "torments" men for five months. In the Iraq war, allied casualties were very light, almost minimal. (It was actually more dangerous to be on the streets of a major U.S. city than in combat against the Iraqi army.) There were a few thousand deaths caused by the Iraqi army, but compared to the carnage of other wars involving such large numbers of soldiers it was very small. The torment could very easily refer to the occupation of Kuwait and the torment of its citizens.

6. Men will want to die but death shall flee from them during these days. During times of starvation and plagues and warfare it is common for people to want to die, and yet they will keep barely hanging on, surviving day by day. This could accurately describe both the past situation during the Kuwait occupation, during the war itself, and even the current situation in Iraq which will last a while longer.

If the above Gulf War is the war described by John (and the peculiar similarities match so well as to not believe otherwise), then this again serves to indicate how close the Savior's coming truly is. The Bible then goes on to say:

> *"One woe is past; and, behold, there come two woes more hereafter."*

John then goes on to describe a terrible war, very much unlike the previous war, except that again it appears to use modern weapons.

LAST PLAGUE #6
MORE DEVASTATING WARS...
THE SECOND "WOE"

A 13 Month World War

> *Rev 9:13-21...* *"And the sixth angel sounded and I heard a voice from the four horns of the golden altar which is before God,*
> *"Saying to the sixth angel which had the trumpet, Loose the four angels which are bound in the great river Euphrates.*
> *"And the four angels were loosed, which were prepared for an hour, and a day, and a month, and a year, for to slay the third part of men.*
> *"And the number of the army of the horsemen were two hundred thousand thousand: and I heard the number of them.*
> *"And thus I saw the horses in the vision, and them that sat on them, having breastplates of fire, and of jacinth, and brimstone: and the heads of the horses were as the heads of lions; and out of their mouths issued fire and smoke and brimstone.*
> *"By these three was the third part of men killed, by the fire, and by the smoke, and by the brimstone, which issued out of their mouths.*
> *"For their power is in their mouth and in their tails: for their tails were like unto serpents, and had heads, and with them they do hurt.*
> *"And the rest of the men which were not killed by these plagues*

yet repented not of the works of their hands, that they should not worship devils, and idols of gold, and silver, and brass, and stone, and of wood: which neither can see, nor hear, nor walk:

"Neither repented they of their murders, nor of their sorceries, nor of their fornication, nor of their thefts."

Rev 16:12-14,16... "And the sixth angel poured out his vial upon the great river Euphrates; and the water thereof was dried up, that the way of the kings of the east might be prepared.

"And I saw three unclean spirits like frogs come out of the mouth of the dragon, and out of the mouth of the beast, and out of the mouth of the false prophet.

"For they are the spirits of devils, working miracles, which go forth unto the kings of the earth and of the whole world, to gather them to the battle of that great day of God Almighty.

"And he gathered them together into a place called in the Hebrew tongue Armageddon."

Again, another plague with a specific time frame for completion (1 year + 1 month + 1 day + 1 hour). The armies of this second war total 200,000,000 strong and engage in a tremendous world war that lasts for just over thirteen months. Reportedly, the third part of men are killed. This would leave an estimated almost 2 billion dead. Again, this war is apparently fought with modern weapons.

There are so many questions concerning such an army, the first of which is where do all the members of this army and their weapons come from? If all of the armies in the world were combined together it would not total 50,000,000, let alone 200 million. To get an idea of the magnitude of such an army, there are approximately 260,000,000 inhabitants in the U.S. and approximately 280,000,000 in the former Soviet Union. Such an army would have to consist of not only regular army personnel, but citizens of perhaps several countries who have been armed for such a war. In the scriptures, such additional detail is not forthcoming. However, there is perhaps an additional credible witness and prophecy of this future world war, particularly as it affects the United States.

GEORGE WASHINGTON'S VISION OF A FUTURE DEVASTATING WAR IN AMERICA

(Note: Even though this is not a Biblical reference, I strongly felt I needed to include this here as part of the discussion concerning this terrible world war. It sheds tremendous light on perhaps how this war will affect the United States and its people. It is of extreme interest that President Washington, a deeply religious and prayerful man, indicates that the force that comes against the United States is the whole world, but is lead primarily by forces from Europe, Asia and Africa. Note, also, that after a tremendous war, the people of the United States are finally victorious.)

In 1777, while in the terrible winter of Valley Forge, the great "father" of the United States, George Washington, recorded in his journal a visitation he had by an "angel," who showed to him in vision the destiny of the United States.

"And again I heard the mysterious voice saying, 'Son of the Republic, look and learn.' At this the dark, shadowy angel placed a trumpet to his mouth, and blew three distinct blasts; and taking water from the ocean he sprinkled it upon Europe, Asia and Africa. Then my eyes beheld a fearful scene: from each of these countries arose thick, black clouds that were soon joined into one. Throughout this mass there gleamed a dark red light by which I saw hordes of armed men, who, moving with the cloud, marched by land and sailed by sea to America. Our country was enveloped in this volume of cloud, and I saw these vast armies devastate the whole country and burn the villages, towns and cities that I beheld springing up. As my ears listened to the thundering of the cannon, clashing of swords, and the shouts and cries of millions in mortal combat, I heard the mysterious voice saying, 'Son of the Republic, look and learn.' When the voice had ceased, the dark shadowy angel placed his trumpet once more to his mouth, and blew a long and fearful blast.

"Instantly a light as of a thousand suns shone down from above me, and pierced and broke into fragments the dark cloud which enveloped America. That same moment the angel upon whose head still shone the word Union, and who bore our national flag in one hand and a sword in the other, descended from the heavens attended by legions of white spirits. These immediately joined the inhabitants of America, who I perceived were well nigh overcome, but who immediately taking courage again, closed up their broken ranks and renewed the battle.

"Again, amid the fearful noise of the conflict, I heard the mysterious voice saying, 'Son of the Republic, look and learn.' As the voice ceased, the shadowy angel for the last time dipped water from the ocean and sprinkled it upon America. Instantly the dark cloud rolled back, together with the armies it had brought, leaving the inhabitants of the land victorious!

"Then once more I beheld the villages, towns and cities springing up where I had seen them before, while the bright angel, planting the azure standard he had brought in the midst of them, cried with a loud voice: 'While the stars remain, and the heavens send down the dew upon the earth, so long shall the Union last.' And taking from his brow the crown on which blazoned the word 'Union,' he placed it upon the Standard while the people, kneeling down, said, 'Amen.'

"The scene instantly began to fade and dissolve, and I at last saw nothing but the rising, curling vapor I had at first beheld. This also disappearing, I found myself once more gazing upon the mysterious visitor, who, in the same voice I had heard before, said, 'Son of the Republic, what you have seen is thus interpreted: Three great perils will come upon the Republic. The most fearful is the third, but in this greatest conflict the whole world united shall not prevail against her. Let every child of the Republic learn to live for his God, his land and the Union. With these words the vision vanished, and I started from my seat and felt that I had seen a vision wherein had been shown to me the birth, progress, and destiny of the United States."[1]

This world war is only the beginning of the sixth plague or the 2nd Woe. Many more catastrophic events occur as part of the sixth plague. They are discussed in a possible order of occurrence as they lead up to the 7th and final plague, the 3rd Woe....which at the end, is the actual appearance of the Savior to the world.

---

[1] *"George Washington's Vision And Prophecy For America"* John Grady, M.D. Route 2 Box 165 Benton, TN 37307

THE LAST BATTLE AT ARMAGEDDON

After this 13 month war, the remnants of this tremendous army that has been gathered, fail to repent of their wickedness and march towards Jerusalem to become involved in the final battle called the battle of Armageddon. Along the way they are joined by other armies to the point that this army becomes innumerable. Miracles are performed by the "false prophet" and the devil, which continues to inflame and drive this army. This army apparently comes from the north and east of Jerusalem because one of the miracles that is performed is that the great river Euphrates is dried up so that this vast army can proceed towards its goal of utter destruction.

A few prophetic accounts exist of this great army, along with the other armies that join it, and their subsequent gathering to Armageddon.[1] (Armageddon means "Mountain of Megiddo" and refers to a valley where many ancient battles have taken place. The valley of Megiddo is about 50 miles north of Jerusalem.)

Ezekiel has some very descriptive language concerning this army and it's appearance. (See Ezekiel 38:1-23)

> "And the word of the Lord came unto me, saying,
> "Son of man, set thy face against Gog, the land of Magog, the chief prince of Meshech and Tubal, and prophesy against him,
> "And say, Thus saith the Lord God; Behold, I am against thee, O Gog, the chief prince of Meshech and Tubal:
> "And I will turn thee back, and put hooks into thy jaws, and I will bring thee forth, and all thine army, horses and horsemen, all of them clothed with all sorts of armour, even a great company with bucklers and shields, all of them handling swords:
> "Persia, Ethiopa, and Libya with them; all of them with shield and helmet:
> "Gomer, and all his bands; the house of Togarmah of the north quarters, and all his bands: and many people with thee.

---

[1] In Joel the apparent movements and conflicts of this army or these last series of battles, as well as brief descriptions of conflicts that precede it are described. Please see the review of the vision of Joel at the end of the book in the Appendix section.

"Be thou prepared, and prepare for thyself, thou, and all thy company that are assembled unto thee, and be thou a guard unto them.

"After many days thou shalt be visited: in the latter years thou shalt come into the land that is brought back from the sword, and is gathered out of many people, against the mountains of Israel, which have been always waste: but it is brought forth out of the nations, and they shall dwell safely all of them.

"Thou shalt ascend and come like a storm, thou shalt be like a cloud to cover the land, thou, and all thy bands, and many people with thee.

"Thus saith the Lord God; It shall also come to pass, that at the same time shall things come into thy mind, and thou shalt think an evil thought:

"And thou shalt say, I will go up to the land of unwalled villages; I will go to them that are at rest, that dwell safely, all of them dwelling without walls, and having neither bars nor gates,

"To take a spoil, and to take a prey; to turn thine hand upon the desolate places that are now inhabited, and upon the people that are gathered out of the nations, which have gotten cattle and goods, that dwell in the midst of the land.

"And thou shalt come from thy place out of the north parts, thou, and many people with thee, all of them riding upon horses, a great company, and a mighty army:

"And thou shalt come up against my people of Israel, as a cloud to cover the land; it shall be in the latter days, and I will bring thee against my land, that the heathen may know me, when I shall be sanctified in thee, O Gog, before their eyes.

"And it shall come to pass at the same time when Gog shall come against the land of Israel, saith the Lord God, that my fury shall come up in my face.

"And I will call for a sword against him throughout all my mountains, saith the Lord God: every man's sword shall be against his brother.

"And I will plead against him with pestilence and with blood; and I will rain upon him, and upon his bands, and upon the many people that are with him, an overflowing rain, and great hailstones, fire, and brimstone.

"Thus will I magnify myself, and sanctify myself; and I will be known in the eyes of many nations, and they shall know that I am the Lord."[1]

In the Revelation Chapter Sixteen reference, it is the "Kings of the East" who come leading their armies across the river Euphrates. They are then joined by the kings of the earth. In Ezekiel's prophetic account the following are named:

*Persia (modern day Turkey/Iraq/Iran/Syria),
*Ethiopia (Egypt),
*Libya (Libya/Algeria),
*Magog-Mesech (Ukraine/Russia/Hungary/Poland/Romania),
*Togarmah (Georgia/Kazakhstan/Russia),
*Sheba (Arabia),
*Dedan (A city of Arabia)
*Tarshish (Spain/Southern France)
*Tubal (Greece/Bulgaria/Yugoslavia/Albania),
*Gomer (England and Northern Europe)

In Joel 3:4, Tyre and Zidon (Cities of Lebanon) and the coasts of Palestine (Lebanon) are mentioned. All of the kings of the earth are mentioned as composing part of this army, but between the three accounts almost all of the modern day Islamic/Arab states (currently under heavy siege to become part of the extremely militant and violent Islamic Fundamentalist Movement), plus Russia, Greece and almost all of Europe are specifically singled out. In Ezekiel it is the king of Gog and Magog or King Gog, Chief Prince of Meshech (Note: many linguists believe that the name Meshech was later changed to Moscow) of the country of Magog that lead these armies to the battle of Armageddon. Apparently these groups comprise the main part of this Armageddon army. (It is interesting to note the fighting and turmoil currently going on in these areas, along with the combining of Europe/NATO into a single unity.)

---

[1] *Ezekiel 38:1-23*

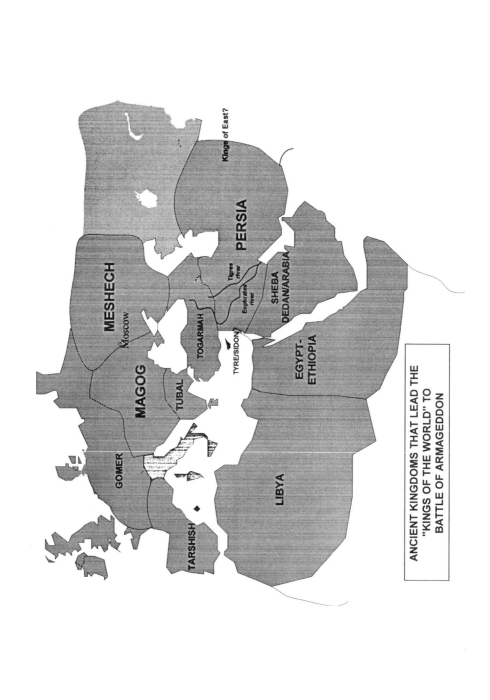

ANCIENT KINGDOMS THAT LEAD THE
"KINGS OF THE WORLD" TO
BATTLE OF ARMAGEDDON

MAP OF ISRAEL

Showing location of major cities, Megiddo and Plain of Esdraelon or the valley of Armageddon

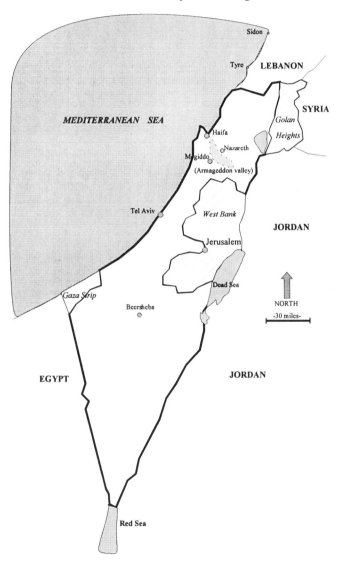

THE ABOMINATION OF DESOLATION

The term "The abomination that maketh desolate", which is mentioned several times in the scriptures,[1] refers to the scene of destruction and desolation that will occur when the Armageddon army reaches Jerusalem and lays siege to it. Daniel the Prophet spoke of a future event when there would be "the abomination that maketh desolate", and the phrase was later used in New Testament times. This event was to happen three times in fulfillment of Daniel's words. The first time was fulfilled when Antiochus IV Epiphanes, laid siege and then looted Jerusalem in 169 B.C.. The second time was when the Roman legions under Titus, in 70 A.D. laid siege to Jerusalem eventually destroying it completely and the third is to be when the Armageddon army begins to do likewise just prior to the Lord's coming. The recorded accounts of the terrible destruction, slaughter, starvation, cannibalism, wickedness, etc. of the Jews in Jerusalem, though the Christians were spared,[2] during the Roman siege makes one cringe, especially in light of the fact that the second abomination of desolation will be even worse.[3] The Savior himself forewarned of this terrible event:

> *"When ye, therefore shall see the abomination of desolation, spoken of by Daniel the prophet, stand in the holy place (whoso readeth, let him understand:)*
> *"Then let them which be in Judea flee into the mountains:*
> *"Let him which is on the housetop not come down to take anything out of his house:*
> *"Neither let him which is in the field return back to take his clothes.*
> *"And woe unto them that are with child, and to them that give suck in those days!*

---

[1] *The term "abomination that maketh desolate" reminded the Jews of the abomination that had happened in 170 B.C. when the Syrian king Antiochus IV massacred the Jews in Jerusalem. See Daniel 9:27, 11:31, 12:11, Matthew 24:15,*

[2] *The Christians were spared because they followed the warning advice that Christ had given earlier to flee when the signs of such destruction began to appear. The early Christian scholar Eusebius wrote: "The whole body, however, of the church at Jerusalem, having been commanded by a divine revelation, given to men of approved piety there before the war, removed from the city, and dwelt at a certain town beyond the Jordan, called Pella." Epiphanes also wrote of this escape: "[as] Vespasian was approaching with his army, all who believed in Christ left Jerusalem and fled to Pella, and other places beyond the river Jordan; and so they all marvelously escaped the general shipwreck of their country: not one of them perished."*

[3] *In the "The Story of Civilization", Will Durant said: the siege of Jerusalem under Titus, lasted for 134 days, during which 1,110,000 Jews perished and 97,000 were taken captive; the Romans destroyed 987 towns in Palestine and slew 580,000 men, and a still larger number, we are told, perished through starvation, disease, and fire.*

"But pray ye that your flight be not in the winter, neither on the sabbath day;

"For then shall be great tribulation, such as was not since the beginning of the world to this time, *no, nor ever shall be.*

"And except those days should be shortened, there should no flesh be saved: but for the elect's sake those days shall be shortened." [1]

The battle for the city of Jerusalem, called the battle of Armageddon, which turns into a complete siege of the city, lasts for 42 months or 3½ years.

"But the court which is without the temple leave out, and measure it not; for it is given unto the Gentiles: **and the holy city shall they tread under foot forty and two months**." [2]

THE GREAT FALSE PROPHET & THE ANTI-CHRIST

In the scriptures there are references to false prophets and false Christs that would be present during the last days. The Savior specifically warned against believing those false teachers/imposters by saying that He would not come as an ordinary man (or a woman), but in a glorious, unmistakable manner from the heavens.

"Then if any man shall say unto you, Lo, here is Christ, or there; believe it not.

"For there shall arise false Christs, and false prophets, and shall shew great signs and wonders; insomuch that, if it were possible, they shall deceive the very elect.

"Behold, I have told you before.

"Wherefore if they shall say unto you, Behold, he is in the desert; go not forth: behold, he is in the secret chambers; believe it not.

---

[1]*Matthew 24:15-22*

[2]*Revelation 11:2-3*

> *"For as the lightning cometh out of the east, and shineth even unto the west; so shall also the coming of the Son of man be."[1]*

> *"And when he had spoken these things, while they beheld, he was taken up; and a cloud received him out of their sight.*
> *"And while they looked stedfastly toward heaven as he went up, behold, two men stood by them in white apparel;*
> *"Which also said, Ye men of Galilee, why stand ye gazing up into heaven? this same Jesus, which is taken up from you into heaven, shall so come in like manner as ye have seen him go into heaven."[2]*

There are also references to a particular great false prophet, which is often referred to as the anti-Christ. Apparently, one of these false prophets rises to the forefront, with great power given him by Satan, which enables him to perform many miracles. Remember, during the time of Moses, the magicians and sorcerers of Pharaoh were able to duplicate several of Moses' miracles, including changing their rods to serpents[3], changing water to blood[4], and bringing frogs up to cover the land[5]. However, they could not duplicate the remainder of the Lord's miracles wrought by Moses.

This great false prophet is only mentioned a few times in the scriptures.

> *"And the beast was taken, and with him the **false prophet that wrought miracles before him, with which he deceived them that had received the mark of the beast, and them that worshipped his image.** These both were cast alive into a lake of fire burning with brimstone."[6]*

> *"And I saw three unclean spirits like frogs come out of the mouth of the dragon, and out of the mouth of the beast, and **out of the***

---

[1] *Matt 24:23-27*

[2] *Acts 1:9-11*

[3] *Ex 7:11*

[4] *Ex 7:22*

[5] *EX 8:7*

[6] *Rev 19:20*

mouth of the false prophet.
"For they are the spirits of devils, working miracles, which go forth unto the kings of the earth and of the whole world, to gather them to the battle of that great day of God Almighty." [1]

This false prophet is apparently associated with, or eventually joins, the kingdom of the beast (Satan's final spiritual/political kingdom) that controls the world at this time and is able to perform powerful miracles to deceive the world. Using these evil miracles that will deceive even some of the elect of God, he gathers the armies of the world together (possibly immediately following the 13 month world war where 1/3 of the world is killed) to march against Israel and Jerusalem in the war called Armageddon.

Again the question might be asked, "If we are so close to the 6th plague, do we see any evidence of such a great false prophet, who is going about the world performing "miracles" and deceiving the world and who might be associated with the kingdom of the beast?" And the answer is, yes, possibly. Below, is a potential candidate who is being promoted by the United Nations. (For additional information, do a WWW search on Maitreya.)

His name is Maitreya and he is reportedly appearing (and later disappearing out of thin air) at different places in the world, surrounded by a blue "glow" and performing miracles. He claims that he is Jesus Christ, the Messiah of the Jews, Krishna, Buddha, and the Imam Mahdi or the Messiah of the Muslims all rolled into one. What follows are a few examples of his publicity as found in the U.N. Share International magazine.

> "He has been expected for generations by all of the major religions. Christians know Him as the Christ, and expect His imminent return. Jews await Him as the Messiah; Hindus look for the coming of Krishna; Buddhists expect Him as Maitreya Buddha; and Muslims anticipate the Imam Mahdi or Messiah.
> "The names may be different, but many believe they all refer to the same individual: the World Teacher, whose name is Maitreya.
> "Preferring to be known simply as the Teacher, Maitreya has not come as a religious leader, or to found a new religion, but as a

---

[1] Rev 16:13-14

teacher and guide for people of every religion and those of no religion.

"At this time of great political, economic and social crises Maitreya will inspire humanity to see itself as one family, and create a civilization based on sharing, economic and social justice, and global cooperation.

"He will launch a call to action to save the millions of people who starve to death every year in a world of plenty. Among Maitreya's recommendations will be a shift in social priorities so that adequate food, housing, clothing, education, and medical care become universal rights.

"Under Maitreya's inspiration, humanity itself will make the required changes and create a saner and more just world for all.

"As a modern man concerned with today's problems, Maitreya has worked on many levels since 1977 to prepare humanity for His outward presence." [He reportedly descended from His ancient retreat in the Himalayas and is now living in London.]

"From behind the scenes, the outpouring of His extraordinary energy has been the stimulus for dramatic changes on many fronts, including the fall of communism in the Soviet Union, the collapse of apartheid in South Africa, the rapprochement between East and West, the growing power of the people's voice, and a worldwide focus on preserving the environment.

"Since 1988 Maitreya has appeared miraculously throughout the world, mainly to orthodox religious groups, presenting in the simplest terms the great spiritual laws governing our lives. And, through steadily increasing signs and spiritual manifestations, now widely reported in the media, He has touched the hearts of millions, preparing them for His imminent appearance.

At the earliest possible moment, Maitreya will demonstrate His true identity on the Day of Declaration."[1]

---

[1]*See Share International magazine, or www.shareintl.org*

THE TWO PROPHETS OF JERUSALEM

As opposites to the great false prophet who is to come forth and gather the armies of the world to the battle of Armageddon, during the time of this final battle there are apparently two true humble prophets who prophesy in Jerusalem for approximately 3½ years, and by miraculous means keep the tremendous Armageddon Army from overrunning Jerusalem while they complete their ministry. (Zechariah also mentions the *"two olive trees."* See Zech 4:11-14)

As Moses called forth plagues, fire and smoke against the armies of Pharaoh and Elijah called down fire from above against the armies of the world in their day, so will these two prophets exercise the Lord's power over the armies and people who come against them. Eventually these two prophets finish their testimony of Jesus and are allowed to be killed after almost 3 ½ years (1260 days). The world rejoices over their deaths, even sending each other gifts while their bodies are left unburied in the street. However, 3½ days after their deaths, the spirit of life re-enters their bodies and they stand up. A voice from heaven then says, "Come up hither" and they ascend up to heaven in a cloud. Then, within the hour, the seventh and final plague begins.[1]

> *"And I will give power unto my two witnesses, and they shall prophesy a **thousand two hundred and threescore days**, clothed in sackcloth.*
>
> *"These are the two olive trees, and the two candlesticks standing before the God of the earth.*
>
> ***"And if any man will hurt them, fire proceedeth out of their mouth, and devoureth their enemies: and if any man will hurt them, he must in this manner be killed.***
>
> ***"These have power to shut heaven, that it rain not in the days of their prophecy: and have power over waters to turn them to blood, and to smite the earth with all plagues, as often as they will.***
>
> *"And when they shall have finished their testimony, the beast that ascendeth out of the bottomless pit shall make war against them, and shall overcome them, and kill them.*
>
> ***"And their dead bodies shall lie in the street of the great city, which spiritually is called Sodom and Egypt, where also our Lord***

---

[1] *In the Rev 11:13-15 account, this great earthquake occurs at the end of the sixth plague. In the Rev 16:17-21 account, it occurs at the beginning of the seventh plague. At this point when things are happening so quickly it is hard to distinguish where one plague stops and another begins.*

was crucified.

"And they of the people and kindreds and tongues and nations shall see their dead bodies three days and an half, and shall not suffer their dead bodies to be put in graves.

"And they that dwell upon the earth shall rejoice over them, and make merry, and shall send gifts one to another; because these two prophets tormented them that dwelt on the earth.

"And after three days and an half the Spirit of life from God entered into them, and they stood upon their feet; and great fear fell upon them which saw them.

"And they heard a great voice from heaven saying unto them, Come up hither. And they ascended up to heaven in a cloud; and their enemies beheld them.

"And the same hour was there a great earthquake, and the tenth part of the city fell, and in the earthquake were slain of men seven thousand: and the remnant were affrighted, and gave glory to the God of heaven.

"The second woe is past; and, behold, the third woe cometh quickly."[1]

It is incredible to consider that the relatively small armies of Israel, backed only by the miracles of these two humble prophets testifying of Christ to the Jews, could possibly withstand the onslaught of the greatest army ever assembled in the history of the world, over 200,000,000 strong for 3 ½ years before finally being overcome. No wonder the evil and wicked people of the world celebrate when their frustrations are completed and they finally kill these two prophets. But again imagine their unbelief, turning-to-fear, when they stand up and then rise to heaven. Immediately following this, within the hour, John says a very great worldwide earthquake occurs.

---

[1]*Revelations 11:3-14*

LAST PLAGUE #7
THE BEGINNING OF THE THIRD
AND FINAL "WOE"

A TREMENDOUS EARTHQUAKE

Rev 16:17-20... "And the seventh angel poured out his vial into the air; and there came a great voice out of the temple of heaven, from the throne, saying, It is done.

"And there were voices, and thunders, and lightnings: and there was a great earthquake, such as was not since men were upon the earth, so mighty an earthquake, and so great.

"And the great city was divided into three parts, and the cities of the nations fell: and great Babylon came in rememberence before God, to give unto her the cup of the wine of the fierceness of his wrath.

"And every island fled away, and the mountains were not found."

A tremendous earthquake is described here as well as in the previous scripture, one in which all of the cities of the earth are destroyed or severely damaged, that levels mountains and makes islands disappear. Specifically in Jerusalem, the earthquake splits the city into three parts; a tenth of the city is completely destroyed and 7,000 immediately die from it's effects.

Also, according to John in Revelation Chapters 17 and 18, the great evil city, spiritually called "Babylon," which *"reigneth over the kings of the earth"* and is a part of the "beast," or the Devil's kingdom, and to whom the ten kingdoms/Europe give their power to for a while, will also be destroyed and catch fire. Europe eventually goes against this great city built on *"seven mountains"* which for a time had dominion over *"peoples, and multitudes, and nations and tongues"* and which made *"war with the Lamb." "Therefore shall her plagues come in one day, death, and mourning, and famine; and she shall be utterly burned with fire: for strong is the Lord God who judgeth her."*

83

What great evil city these scriptures refer to is not clear. It is definitely not Jerusalem, which had been called Babylon occasionally, because this evil city will be forever barren and desolate after it is destroyed *"in one hour."* The Lord considered this a very evil city because, *"for by thy sorceries were all nations deceived. And in her was found the blood of prophets, and of saints, and of all that were slain upon the earth."[1]* This is probably another example wherein we will find out what city this is referring to after this event takes place.

In Ezekiel 38:18-20 and other scriptures this great earthquake is also described;

> *"And it shall come to pass at the same time when Gog shall come against the land of Israel, saith the Lord God, that my fury shall come up in my face.*
> *"For in my jealousy and in the fire of my wrath have I spoken, Surely in that day there shall be a great shaking in the land of Israel;*
> *"So that the fishes of the sea, and the fowls of the heaven, and the beasts of the field, and all creeping things that creep upon the earth, and **all the men that are upon the face of the earth, shall shake at my presence, and the mountains shall be thrown down, and the steep places shall fall, and every wall shall fall to the ground."***
>
> *"For thus saith the Lord of hosts; Yet once, it is a little while, and I will shake the heavens, and the earth, and the sea, and the dry land;*
> *"And I will shake all nations,"[2]*

What would cause such an earthquake? Perhaps a huge meteorite striking the earth in one of it's oceans, or perhaps the moon, causing the earth to shift in it's orbit? Nevertheless, how or what causes this tremendous earthquake, the consequences of it are monumental. In fact, John mentions that the location of the islands are moved... to the point of it being called a new earth. A change in the earths's orbit would give the heavens a completely new look. Isaiah, also mentions both of these events a few times as well as Peter:

---

[1] *Rev 18:17,18,23,24*

[2] *Haggai 2:6-7*

"And every mountain and island were moved out of their places." [1]

"For, behold, I create new heavens and a new earth: and the former shall not be remembered, nor come into mind."
"For as the new heavens and the new earth, which I will make, *shall remain before me, saith the LORD, so shall your seed and your name remain."* [2]

"Nevertheless we, according to his promise, **look for new heavens and a new earth,** *wherein dwelleth righteousness."* [3]

There are some old legends and stories associated with the Tower of Babel and the flood that indicate that at one time all of the land masses of the earth were joined together. The scriptures also seem to indicate that this perhaps was the case because it mentions a point in which the earth became divided:

"And unto Eber were born two sons: the name of one was Peleg; for in his days was the earth divided;" [4]

It is interesting to note that most modern day scientists believe that the evidence strongly indicates that at one time this actually had been the case. It is called the Continental Drift Theory, because the continents are actually floating...drifting... land masses resting on the liquid core of the earth and are still actually moving, albeit, very, very slowly.   It is not too far fetched to consider that a large meteor striking the earth could cause the continents to shift, causing in effect a *"new earth"* and the earth's orbit or axis to change as well giving rise to *"new heavens."*

The idea of a meteorite or meteorites striking the earth is also strongly hinted of in the scriptures. John described it thus:

---

[1] *Rev 6:14*

[2] *Isaiah 65:17; 66:22*

[3] *2 Peter 3:13*

[4] *Genesis 10:25*

> *"and the stars of heaven fell unto the earth, even as a fig tree casteth her untimely figs when she is shaken of a mighty wind."*[1]

Though traumatic as such an event would be, however, the Savior still has not come yet to the world. How long between this earth shattering earthquake and the Savior's coming is not specified, but it appears to be somewhat short. Just long enough for the majority of people generally to not repent, but to try and hide and cringe from the wrath of God during the resulting chaos.

> *"and, lo, there was a great earthquake; and the sun became black as sackcloth of hair, and the moon became as blood,*
>
> *"And the stars of heaven fell unto the earth, even as a fig tree casteth her untimely figs, when she is shaken of a mighty wind.*
>
> *"And the heaven departed as a scroll when it is rolled together; and every mountain and island were moved out of their places.*
>
> *"And the kings of the earth, and the great men, and the rich men, and the chief captains, and the mighty men, and every bondman, and every free man, hid themselves in the dens and in the rocks of the mountains,*
>
> *"And said to the mountains and rocks, Fall on us, and hide us from the face of him that sitteth on the throne, and from the wrath of the Lamb,"*[2]

A TREMENDOUS PLAGUE OF HAIL

According to several references, many already quoted above, there is a great plague of hail or hailstones that immediately follows this cataclysmic earthquake. John mentions this plague of hail twice, in Rev 11:19 and then in more detail in Rev 16:21

> *"And the temple of God was opened in heaven, and there was seen in his temple the ark of his testament: and there were lightnings, and voices, and thunderings, and an earthquake, and great hail."*

---

[1] *Rev 6:13*

[2] *Rev 6:12-17*

> *"And there fell upon men a great hail out of heaven, every stone about the weight of a talent: and men blasphemed God because of the plague of the hail; for the plague thereof was exceeding great."*

A talent weighs approximately 72-76 lbs. It is almost impossible to imagine a global hailstorm wherein the stones were 72 lbs. If one imagines a hailstorm of bowling balls, it is indeed a terrible thought. But bowling balls only average about 12-16 lbs...these future hailstones are six times the size of bowling balls. No wonder John says that the wicked blasphemed God because the plague of the hail was exceeding great.

Isaiah mentions hail a few times when referring to the last days, but not more than in a general way. (See Is 28:2,17) Ezekiel also mentions this great plague of hail, along with fire and brimestone:

> *"And I will plead against him with pestilence and with blood; and I will rain upon him, and upon his bands, and upon the many people that are with him, an overflowing rain, **and great hailstones, fire, and brimstone.**"*[1]

It is important to note that in Exodus 9:24-26, Moses called down a very similarly grievous hailstorm (mixed with fire) the like that had never been experienced in Egypt since it's beginning. The hail destroyed everything, cattle, trees, crops, etc. except in the land of Goshen among the children of Israel who were spared the plague of the hail. Perhaps this future hailstorm will also spare those righteous who are gathered together in the name of Jesus.

Interestingly, Ezekiel mentions fire and brimstone with the hail very similar to the hail of Moses which brought fire. Perhaps this hail could also possibly refer to rocks or meteorites coming down from the sky. If the great earthquake was caused by a large meteor, large rocks falling or accompanying the large meteor, or as a result of the impact would make logical sense. The next event also lends a little more credence to the meteorite/comet interpretation as well.

---

[1] *Ezekiel 38:22*

ALL LIFE IN THE SEA DIES

As a possible consequence or side effect of this tremendous global earthquake that destroys the cities of the world, John mentions that all of the life in the sea dies. This is mentioned as part of the seven last plagues, and is perhaps the final conclusion to 1/3 of the life in the sea dying. Also, as part of the second general plague, 1/3 of the ships in the sea were destroyed. If the great earthquake were indeed caused by a large meteorite, or "*falling star*," hitting the earth, it would be very easily understood how the ships in the sea would be destroyed along with the life in the oceans dying.

> *"And the second angel poured out his vial upon the sea; and it became as the blood of a dead man: and every living soul died in the sea."[1]*

This idea of great tribulations of the sea is mentioned elsewhere as well. Ezekiel mentions that when the great wicked city of Babylon is destroyed in the last days, it is covered by the sea. Luke also mentions the sea and the waves roaring.

> *"How is Sheshach taken! and how is the praise of the whole earth surprised! how is Babylon become an astonishment among the nations!*
>
> *"The sea is come up upon Babylon: she is covered with the multitude of the waves thereof.*
>
> *"Her cities are a desolation, a dry land, and a wilderness, a land wherein no man dwelleth, neither doth any son of man pass thereby"*
> [2]

> *"And there shall be signs in the sun, and in the moon, and in the stars; and upon the earth distress of nations, with perplexity; the sea and the waves roaring"[3]*

---

[1]*Rev 16:3*

[2]*Jeremiah 51:41-43*

[3]*Luke 21:25*

THE SAVIOR'S APPEARING TO THE JEWS

The Bible seems to indicate that quickly following this great earthquake, the Jews have a meeting with their Messiah, who is in actuality Jesus Christ, before the Savior makes his glorious appearance to the whole world following the ascending of the righteous living and the righteous dead to heaven. (The "Rapture" will be discussed later.)

Though Jesus does not come to the whole world at this time, He does make an appearance to the Jews left in Jerusalem in the new valley of Mount Olivet or the Mount of Olives which has split in half because of the earthquake.

> *"And his feet shall stand in that day upon the mount of Olives, which is before Jerusalem on the east,* **and the mount of Olives shall cleave in the midst thereof toward the east and toward the west and there shall be a very great valley, and half of the mountain shall remove toward the north, and half of it toward the south.**
>
> *"And ye shall flee to the valley of the mountains; for the valley of the mountains shall reach unto Azal: yea, ye shall flee, like as ye fled from before the earthquake in the days of Uzziah king of Judah: and the Lord my God shall come, and all the saints with thee."* [1]

Again, as the Jews flee the advancing Armageddon army as it goes house to house, raping and pillaging the city of Jerusalem, the remaining Jews flee to the temple mount on the east side of Jerusalem to make a last stand. At this point there is no place to escape to because behind them is the valley Kidron and the Mount of Olives and the innumerable army is before them. At this point the two prophets come alive, ascend into heaven, and the great earthquake and hailstorm occurs. As mentioned before, John says that 7,000 in the city die immediately. Zechariah indicates that two thirds of the Jews die in these events with only one third remaining.

> **"And it shall come to pass, that in all the land, saith the Lord, two parts therein shall be cut off and die; but the third shall be left therein.**
>
> *"And I will bring the third part through the fire, and will refine them as silver is refined, and will try them as gold is tried: they shall*

---

[1] Zech 14:4-5

call on my name, and I will hear them: I will say, It is my people: and they shall say, The Lord is my God.[1]

As a result of this tremendous earthquake, the Mount of Olives splits in half towards the North and South, creating a valley into which the remaining Jews flee into to escape. Zechariah says:

> *"For I will gather all nations against Jerusalem to battle; and the city shall be taken, and the houses rifled, and the women ravished; and half of the city shall go forth into captivity, and the residue of the people shall not be cut off from the city.*
>
> *"Then shall the Lord go forth, and fight against those nations, as when he fought in the day of battle.*
>
> *"And his feet shall stand in that day upon the mount of Olives, which is before Jerusalem on the east, andthe mount of Olives shall cleave in the midst thereof toward the east and toward the west, and there shall be a very great valley; and half of the mountain shall remove toward the north, and half of it toward the south.*
>
> *"And ye shall flee to the valley of the mountains; for the valley of the mountains shall reach unto Azal: yea, ye shall flee, like as ye fled from before the earthquake in the days of Uzziah king of Judah: and the Lord my God shall come, and all the saints with thee.*[2]

As the Jews flee into this newly created valley, they finally meet their Messiah who comes to them:

> *"And one shall say unto him, What are these wounds in thine hands? Then he shall answer, Those with which I was wounded in the house of my friends.*[3]

Here finally the Jews who remain alive from the terrible onslaught of the Armageddon army, the great earthquake, and the plague of hailstones, fall down and worship their long awaited Messiah, who in reality is our Lord Jesus. Then

---

[1] *Zech 13:8-9*

[2] *Zechariah 14:2-5*

[3] *Zech 13:6*

the Lord will finish the destruction of the Armageddon army, of which only 1/6 remains.

> *"And I will turn thee back, and leave but the sixth part of thee, and will cause thee to come up from the north parts, and will bring thee upon the mountains of Israel:"*[1]

> *"And this shall be the plague wherewith the Lord will smite all the people that have fought against Jerusalem; Their flesh shall consume away while they stand upon their feet, and their eyes shall consume away in their holes, and their tongue shall consume away in their mouth.*
> *"And it shall come to pass in that day, that a great tumult from the Lord shall be among them; and they shall lay hold every one on the hand of his neighbour, and his hand shall rise up against the hand of his neighbour."*[2]

THE GREAT SUPPER OF THE GREAT GOD FOR THE FOWLS AND BEASTS OF THE EARTH

With the complete destruction of the innumerable Armageddon army, the great feast or the supper of the great God will take place.

> ***"Thou shalt fall upon the mountains of Israel, thou, and all thy bands, and the people that is with thee: I will give thee unto the ravenous birds of every sort, and to the beasts of the field to be devoured.***
> *"Thou shalt fall upon the open field: for I have spoken it, saith the Lord God."*[3]

> *"And, thou son of man, thus saith the Lord God; Speak unto every feathered fowl, and to every beast of the field, Assemble yourselves,*

---

[1]*Ezek 39:2*

[2]*Zech 14:12-13*

[3]*Ezek 39:4-5*

91

and come; gather yourselves on every side to my sacrifice that I do sacrifice for you, even a great sacrifice upon the mountains of Israel, that ye may eat flesh, and drink blood.

"Ye shall eat the flesh of the mighty, and drink the blood of the princes of the earth, of rams, of lambs, and of goats, of bullocks, all of them fatlings of Bashan.

"And ye shall eat fat till ye be full, and drink blood till ye be drunken, of my sacrifice which I have sacrificed for you.

"Thus ye shall be filled at my table with horses and chariots, with mighty men, and with all men of war, saith the Lord GOD."[1]

John wrote:

"And I saw an angel standing in the sun; and he cried with a loud voice, saying to all the fowls that fly in the midst of heaven, **Come and gather yourselves together unto the supper of the great God;**

"That ye may eat the flesh of kings, and the flesh of captains, and the flesh of mighty men, and the flesh of horses, and of them that sit on them, and the flesh of all men, both free and bond, both small and great.

"And I saw the beast, and the kings of the earth, and their armies, gathered together to make war against him that sat on the horse, and against his army.

"And the beast was taken, and with him the false prophet that wrought miracles before him, with which he deceived them that had received the mark of the beast, and them that worshipped his image. These both were cast alive into a lake of fire burning with brimstone.

"And the remnant were slain with the sword of him that sat upon the horse, which sword proceeded *out of his mouth: and all the fowls were filled with their flesh."*

As part of this destruction, Joel says that the Armageddon army (which came from the North), will be driven away from Jerusalem to be destroyed in a barren and desolate land. He also indicates that Egypt and Edom (modern day Jordan/Saudi Arabia) will become a desolate wilderness

"But I will remove far off from you the northern army, and will drive him into a land barren and desolate, with his face toward the

---

[1]*Ezek 39:17-20*

east sea, and his hinder part toward the utmost sea, and his stink shall come up, and his ill savour shall come up, because he hath done great things."

"Egypt shall be a desolation, and Edom shall be a desolate wilderness, for the violence against the children of Judah, because they have shed innocent blood in their land."[1]

Ezekiel indicates that it takes seven months to bury the dead from this battle, with people who have continual employment during a thousand years of the millennium seeking out the bones of the dead in the desert to properly bury them. They burn the fuel and the instruments of war for seven years, without the need for any other source of fuel. (See Ezekiel 39:9-16)

VOICES IN THE HEAVENS

Apparently as part of the events just immediately prior to the Savior's coming, voices are heard from the heavens

"And the seventh angel sounded; and there were great voices in heaven, saying, The kingdoms of this world are become the kingdoms of our Lord, and of his Christ, and he shall reign for ever and ever."[2]

"and the angel took the censer, and filled it with fire of the altar, and cast it unto the earth: and there were voices, and thunderings, and lightnings, and an earthquake."[3]

Specifically we read that there is a voice from heaven that calls up the two witnesses in Jerusalem, after their bodies have laid in the streets for 3 ½ days.

"And they heard a great voice from heaven saying unto them,

---

[1] *Joel 2:20, 3:19*

[2] *Rev 11:15*

[3] *Rev 8:5*

> *Come up hither. And they ascended up to heaven in a cloud; and their enemies beheld them."*[1]

Voices from heaven is nothing completely new, but perhaps just unusually rare. We read in the New Testament that during the life of the Savior upon the earth there were occasionally voices heard from heaven. (See Luke 3:22) As part of the events just prior to the Savior's return, there again appears to be voices from heaven that are heard worldwide.

A NEW TEMPLE IN JERUSALEM
A NEW RIVER FLOWS

In Ezekiel Chapters 40--46, the construction and ordinances of a new temple that will be built in Jerusalem in the last days is described. The construction of this temple is the focus of considerable debate and action in Israel currently. There are two major problems with building what would be the third Jewish temple:

1. The Dome of the Rock, Mosque. This problem is that the site that the temple is to be built upon is the current location of one of the most sacred of all Islamic mosques, the Dome of the Rock , or the reputed place where Mohammed ascended up to heaven. Next to it is the Al-Aqsa mosque, another holy shrine of the Islamic world.

2. The Red Heifer and the Waters of Separation. According to Jewish law (see Numbers 19:2-7), any faithful Jew who has been associated with death is "unclean." In order to be "clean" they must be sprinkled with the "waters of separation" which is made from the ashes of a three year old red heifer. After the Six-day War, in which the Jews gained control of the Temple Mount, the chief rabbis ruled that it was forbidden to enter the Temple Mount area without being cleansed by this *"water of separation,"* since all had been involved with the war and therefore had become *"unclean."* [2] There is some disagreement in whether it means the whole

---

[1]*Rev 11:12*

[2]*Numbers 19:10-17*

Temple Mount or just the location where the Temple once stood, but primarily because of political reasons, Israel does not allow Jews to pray on the Temple Mount. The problem has been that neither a red heifer nor the *"waters of separation"* have been in Israel for almost 2000 years... that is until recently.

RED HEIFER CALF BORN IN ISRAEL

A few quotes from various sources will provide a better background of information:

> *"The birth of a red heifer in Israel is being hailed by religious Jews as a sign from God that work can soon begin on building the Third Temple in Jerusalem.*
>
> *"A team of rabbinical experts last week confirmed that the animal, born six months ago on a religious kibbutz near the Israeli port of Haifa, meets the correct Biblical criteria for a genuine holy cow. According to the Book of Numbers (XIX:2-7), the animal is needed for an ancient Jewish purification ritual.*
>
> *"The heifer will be slaughtered and burned, and its ashes made into a liquid paste and used in a ceremony which religious Jews believe they must undergo before they can enter the old Temple site in Jerusalem to start building a new structure. Since Herod's Temple was destroyed by the Roman Emperor Titus in AD 70, no flawless red heifer has been born within the biblical land of Israel, according to rabbinical teaching.*
>
> *"The birth of the animal, to a black-and-white mother and a dun-coloured bull, is being hailed as a "miracle" by activists who want to rebuild the Third Temple and prepare the way for the Jewish Messiah's entry to Jerusalem. The faithful will need to wait until the heifer is at least three before it can be used in a ritual sacrifice. That would enable religious Jews to start the new millennium (a Christian event, but still regarded as portentous) in a state of purity."* [1]

---

[1] *International News article, 16 March 1997, issue 660, by Con Coughlin in Jerusalem. See also article in Newsweek, April 19, 1997 edition. Do WWW search on "red heifer"*

> *"Jewish theology and tradition state that when the tenth perfect red heifer is born, it is prophetically the time for rebuilding the temple and the Messiah's appearing. The ninth heifer was born 2000 years ago and presently the tenth has arrived in our generation. The Orthodox Jews are now waiting 18 months to see if there are any defects in the animal."* [1]

> *"The Red Heifer, according to oral tradition recorded in the Mishnah, must: be the firstborn of its mother and have no blemishes... be totally red in color... never been yoked or put to work.*
> *"Mishnaic tradition states that from the time of Moses to the destruction of the Second Temple, there were nine heifers. The great Jewish scholar Maimonides said, "...and the tenth heifer will be accomplished by the king, the Messiah; may he be revealed speedily, Amen, May it be God's will."* [2]

Jewish terrorists have tried to destroy the mosques (most notably in 1985), but so far the Israeli police/army has been able to prevent this. In 1990 a group, "The Temple Mount Faithful," tried to ascend the mount to lay a cornerstone for the Third Temple, but were prevented by the police and thousands of Muslims rioting on the Mount and at the Western Wall. However, the birth of the red heifer is being looked upon as a "sign from God" and is uniting many of the Jews as never before concerning building the Third Temple. The Arab nations, on the other hand, are also being united as never before against the Jews, saying that Jewish talk of demolishing the Dome of the Rock and building the Jewish Temple is tantamount to a declaration of war. Many of the Arab nations have begun war preparations.

It is interesting to note that the red heifer will be three years old a few months prior to the year 2000, and many are indicating that immediately following Passover, on April 20, 2000 would be the perfect time to sacrifice the heifer and make the *"waters of separation."* Perhaps on May 7, 2000 which is the traditional day that Solomon and Ezra began building the 1st and 2nd Jewish temples respectively. The calf will be sacrificed on the Mount of Olives, east of the temple mount, and some of its blood will be sprinkled towards the temple site. It is also

---

[1]*News from Israel, Van Impe Intelligence Briefing, June 1997*

[2]*Deseret News, "Blessed Calf" by Karen Boren, pg E1, 6/15/97*

important to note that the Temple Institute of Jerusalem is already in the process of crafting the solid gold and silver vessels needed for temple service. As a safety precaution against the possibility of a premature death of the original red heifer, a few other qualified red heifers have been located and are being kept in reserve.

(Update note: This first red heifer developed three white hairs and was disqualified by the rabbis. However, a second red heifer has been miraculously provided by a gentile in the United States, which has been certified eligible by the Rabbis. It will also be three years old just prior to the Passover in the year 2000.)

The Bible very clearly indicates that somehow, someway, the 3[d] Jewish temple is finally built on the temple mount. (Perhaps it is this that sparks the war that is called Armageddon and the siege of Jerusalem.) It is after this new Jewish temple is built, after 3 ½ years of war that this tremendous, global earthquake is felt. Very soon after the great earthquake, water begins to flow from underneath this new Jewish temple, becoming a great and mighty pure river which heals the Dead Sea.

> *"Afterward he brought me again unto the door of the house; and, behold, **waters issued out from under the threshold of the house eastward**: for the forefront of the house stood toward the east, and the waters came down from under from the right side of the house, at the **south side of the altar**.*
>
> *"Then brought he me out of the way of the gate northward, and led me about the way without unto the utter gate by the way that looketh eastward; and, behold, there ran out waters on the right side.*
>
> *"Afterward he measured a thousand; and it was a river that I could not pass over: **for the waters were risen, waters to swim in , a river that could not be passed over**.*
>
> *"Then said he unto me, **These waters issue out toward the east country, and go down into the desert, and go into the sea: which being brought forth into the sea, the waters shall be healed.**"* [1]

---

[1]*Ezekiel 47:1-2, 5, 8*

SUN DARKENED/MOON TURNED TO BLOOD/ STARS FALL FROM HEAVEN

The timing of the sun being darkened, the moon turning to blood, and the stars falling from heaven as described in Revelations 6:12-17, apparently happens immediately after the cataclysmic earthquake, though, because of the smoke from wars and other events, the sun has been darkened during the last three "woes" or plagues.

A potential fulfillment to the moon turning to blood has often times been described as what the moon looks like through smoke, etc., and has been thought of as just an atmospheric condition. But the references go one step further and declare that not only will the moon be darkened along with the sun and the stars, but that the moon will be turned into blood or will become blood.

> *"The sun shall be turned into darkness, and the moon into blood, before that great and notable day of the Lord come"*[1]

> *"Lo, there was a great earthquake; and the sun became black as sackcloth of hair, and the moon became as blood."*[2]

> *"The sun shall be turned into darkness, and the moon into blood, before the great and the terrible day of the Lord come."*[3]

What does it mean that the moon will be *"turned into blood"*? Does it mean that the moon somehow will cause bloodshed, or that there will be bloodshed on the moon, or, again, is it simply a reference to an atmospheric condition? In other references of Blood, it is used as a general term meaning a great deal of death and destruction. At this point in time, there just is not enough information to clearly understand what is meant by this reference. Only time will tell.

---

[1]*Acts 2:20*

[2]*Rev 6:12*

[3]*Joel 2:31*

NO DARKNESS AT NIGHTTIME

Another sign is mentioned here which again would strike terror in the hearts of the wicked.

> *"And it shall come to pass in that day, that the light shall not be clear, nor dark.*
> *"But it shall be one day which shall be known to the Lord, not day, nor night: but it shall come to pass, that at evening time it shall be light."* [1]

With all of the dust and smoke, etc. in the air during this time from all of the natural calamities and war, a very good description of the daytime light would be *"that the light shall not be clear, nor dark"*. But imagine the consternation of the world when at night, when it should become totally dark, the darkness doesn't come.

THE GREAT SIGN OF THE COMING OF THE SON OF MAN

The great world earthquake helps us place another important event....that of the great or last sign of the coming of the Son of Man:

> *"And, then shall appear the sign of the Son of man in heaven, and then shall all the tribes of the earth mourn; and they shall see the Son of man coming in the clouds of heaven, with power and great glory,"* [2]

> *"And then shall they see the Son of man coming in a cloud with power and great glory."* [3]

Perhaps this Great Sign of the Son of Man, which will be seen by all men together and could appear as a planet or comet, will be so bright that it's appearance will turn night into day as described in Zachariah.   Jude mentions that when the Lord

---

[1] *Zech. 14:6-7*

[2] *Matthew 24:30*

[3] *Luke 21:27*

comes, he will be accompanied with an extremely large group of saints/angels.

> *"And Enoch also, the seventh from Adam, prophesied of these,*
> *saying, **Behold, the Lord cometh with ten thousands of his saints,***
> *"To execute judgment upon all, and to convince all that are*
> *ungodly among them of all their ungodly deeds which they have*
> *ungodly committed, and of all their hard speeches which ungodly*
> *sinners have spoken against him."*[1]

As this great group of angels, the city of New Jerusalem and the Glorious Lord approaches the earth, the world could very easily mistakenly believe that it is a comet or some other celestial object and foresees that it is probably going to strike or pass extremely close to the earth causing great fear to strike the hearts of the wicked.

However fear will not be the case with those who have long awaited and prepared for this event, because they will know that it is not a planet or comet coming, but Jesus Christ and all of the hosts of heaven coming to earth as long foretold, bringing an end to the reign of Satan, his hosts and the wicked on the earth.

THE HOLY CITY OF NEW JERUSALEM

Indications are that a wonderful, beautiful city, the city of God called the New Jerusalem will come with Jesus and the angels and then be established on the earth for the thousand years of the millennium. It appears to be different than the old Jerusalem, and is often referred to as Zion. (The old Jerusalem is also referred to as Zion which sometimes makes it confusing.) Not much detail is given in the Bible concerning this fabulous New Jerusalem. Those who live in this city will be called holy, receive a new name from God and dwell with God.

> *"Him that overcometh will I make a pillar in the temple of my God,*
> *and he shall go no more out: and I will write upon him the name of*
> *my God, and the name of the city of my God, which is new*
> *Jerusalem, which cometh down out of heaven from my God: and I*

---

[1] *Jude 1:14*

will write upon him my new name.[1]

"And I John saw the holy city, new Jerusalem, coming down from God out of heaven, prepared as a bride adorned for her husband.

"And I heard a great voice out of heaven saying, Behold, the tabernacle of God is with men, and he will dwell with them, and they shall be his people, and God himself shall be with them, and be their God.[2]

THE RIGHTEOUS LIVING AND THE DEAD ASCEND TO HEAVEN

With tremendous earthquakes, storms, unbelievable hailstorms, devastating wars, life in the seas dying, voices from heaven, the great sign of the Son of man in the sky, night that never comes even though the sun goes down, stars falling, etc., still the people in the world in general are still surviving. The wicked are still *"eating and drinking, marrying and giving in marriage."* Then two final events happen that shake the wicked to their very core. The first event is commonly called, the "Rapture" though this is not based on any Biblical word.

> *"For the Lord himself shall descend from heaven with a shout, with the voice of the archangel, and with the trump of God: and the dead in Christ shall rise first:*
> *"Then we which are alive and remain shall be caught up together with them in the clouds, to meet the Lord in the air: and so shall we ever be with the Lord.*
> *"Wherefore comfort one another with these words."*[3]

Ezekiel had a vision in the which he apparently describes what happens:

> *"The hand of the LORD was upon me, and carried me out in the spirit of the LORD, and set me down in the midst of the valley which was full of bones,*

---

[1]*Revelation 3:12*

[2]*Revelation 21:2-3*

[3]*1 Thessalonians 4:16-18*

"And caused me to pass by them round about: and, behold, there were very many in the open valley; and, lo, they were very dry.

"And he said unto me, Son of man, can these bones live? And I answered, O Lord GOD, thou knowest.

"Again he said unto me, Prophesy upon these bones, and say unto them, O ye dry bones, hear the word of the LORD.

"Thus saith the Lord GOD unto these bones; Behold, I will cause breath to enter into you, and ye shall live:

"And I will lay sinews upon you, and will bring up flesh upon you, and cover you with skin, and put breath in you, and ye shall live; and ye shall know that I am the LORD.

"So I prophesied as I was commanded: and as I prophesied, there was a noise, and behold a shaking, and the bones came together, bone to his bone.

"And when I beheld, lo, the sinews and the flesh came up upon them, and the skin covered them above: *but there was no breath in them.*

"Then said he unto me, Prophesy unto the wind, prophesy, son of man, and say to the wind, Thus saith the Lord GOD; Come from the four winds, O breath, and breathe upon these slain, that they may live.

"So I prophesied as he commanded me, and the breath came into them, and they lived, and stood up upon their feet, an exceeding great army."[1]

According to the Bible, after the graves have been opened and the dead have risen into the air, then the righteous living shall also rise into heaven to meet the Lord in the air. The Savior said the world in general will still be trying to go about their business when this happens:

"But as the days of Noe were, so shall also the coming of the Son of man be.

"For as in the days that were before the flood they were eating and drinking, marrying and giving in marriage, until the day that Noe entered into the ark,

"And knew not until the flood came, and took them all away; so shall also the coming of the Son of man be.

---

[1]*Ezekiel 37:1-10*

"Then shall two be in the field; the one shall be taken, and the other left.

"Two women shall be grinding at the mill; the one shall be taken, and the other left.

"Watch therefore: for ye know not what hour your Lord doth come." [1]

SILENCE IN HEAVEN

After everything that has been going on, with tremendous storms and lightnings, voices coming from the heavens, the sun, moon and stars darkened, the seas roaring, earthquakes, the great sign of Jesus in the sky, a night that doesn't get dark when the sun goes down, the graves opening up and the dead rising to heaven, the righteous also rising to heaven... then all of a sudden it is deathly still. Perhaps, this final last event strikes absolute terror into the hearts of the remaining wicked, because by now they know beyond a shadow of a doubt, that their just judgement is at hand and they have been found wanting. A complete silence for ½ hour will send the wicked to the caves and tops of the mountains, throwing down their gold and silver and precious idols, understanding fully that nothing will save them from their foretold fate.

"And when he had opened the seventh seal, there was silence in heaven about the space of half an hour." [2]

"And the kings of the earth, and the great men, and the rich men, and the chief captains, and the mighty men, and every bondman, and every free man, hid themselves in the dens and in the rocks of the mountains;

"And said to the mountains and rocks, Fall on us, and hide us from the face of him that sitteth on the throne, and from the wrath of the Lamb:

"For the great day of his wrath is come; and who shall be able to stand?" [3]

---

[1]*Matt 24:37-42*

[2]*Revelation 8:1*

[3]*Revelation 6:15-17*

THE END OF THE 3RD "WOE"

When the Lord's Face Is Revealed In Heaven To The World

HE COMES!

Finally, after all of the events that have been prophesied have occurred, the remaining Jews have finally recognized and worshiped Jesus as their long awaited Messiah (making Him their personal Savior and becoming Christians), the righteous dead and living are no longer on the earth but have ascended to heaven to meet our Lord Jesus Christ in the air, and the deathly silence leaves the wicked trembling with fear in their sins, waiting for the inevitable... then HE COMES, for the first time revealing His face in glory to the world. His glorious appearance is so bright and so powerful that it appears to be similar to the sun rising in the East.

> *"For as the lightning cometh out of the east, and shineth even unto the west; so shall also the coming of the Son of man be."* [1]

> *"And, behold, the glory of the God of Israel came from the way of the east: and his voice was like a noise of many waters: and the earth shined with his glory."* [2]

As His glory shines forth upon the corrupt wicked who have rejected His gospel message of peace, kindness, truth, purity and charity, they cannot stand, but are destroyed in a flaming fire of righteous wrath. The Bible is very clear in that every corruptible thing remaining on the earth at this time is destroyed. Even the very elements of the earth will melt, creating a new earth and a new heaven for a thousand years.

---

[1]*Matt. 24:27*

[2]*Ezekiel 43:2*

"And to you who are troubled rest with us, when the Lord Jesus shall be revealed from heaven with his mighty angels,

"In flaming fire taking vengeance on them that know not God, and that obey not the gospel of our Lord Jesus Christ:

"Who shall be punished with everlasting destruction from the presence of the Lord, and from the glory of his power;"[1]

"But the day of the Lord will come as a thief in the night; in the which the heavens shall pass away with a great noise, and the elements shall melt with fervent heat, the earth also and the works that are therein shall be burned up.

"Seeing then that all these things shall be dissolved, what manner of persons ought ye to be in all holy conversation and godliness,

"Looking for and hasting unto the coming of the day of God, wherein the heavens being on fire shall be dissolved, and the elements shall melt with fervent heat?

"Nevertheless we, according to his promise, look for new heavens and a new earth, wherein dwelleth righteousness."[2]

"And then shall that Wicked be revealed, whom the Lord shall consume with the spirit of his mouth, and shall destroy with the brightness of his coming:"[3]

Other ancient prophets also talked about the great burning and fire when the Savior comes:

"But who may abide the day of his coming? and who shall stand when he appeareth? for he is like a refiner's fire, and like fullers' soap:

"And he shall sit, as a refiner and purifier of silver: and he shall purify the sons of Levi, and purge them as gold and silver, that they may offer unto the LORD an offering in righteousness."[4]

---

[1] *2 Thessalonians 1:7-9*

[2] *2 Peter 3:10-13*

[3] *2 Thessalonians 2:8*

[4] *Malachi 3:2-3*

> *"Therefore hath the curse devoured the earth, and they that dwell therein are desolate: therefore the inhabitants of the earth are burned, and few men left."*[1]

WHO WILL BE SAVED?

In several places in the New Testament, Jesus used the parable of the burning of the tares and the burning of the unfruitful tree as an example of what will happen at His coming and who will not survive this glorious event. Jesus very clearly says that not everyone who professes Jesus will actually be saved at that day.

> *"Every tree that bringeth not forth good fruit is hewn down, and cast into the fire.*
> *"Wherefore by their fruits ye shall know them.*
> *"Not every one that saith unto me, Lord, Lord, shall enter into the kingdom of heaven; but he that doeth the will of my Father which is in heaven.*
> *"Many will say to me in that day, Lord, Lord, have we not prophesied in thy name? and in thy name have cast out devils? and in thy name done many wonderful works?*
> *"And then will I profess unto them, I never knew you: depart from me, ye that work iniquity.*
> *"Therefore whosoever heareth these sayings of mine, and doeth them, I will liken him unto a wise man, which built his house upon a rock:"*[2]

Paul echos this same theme in his letter to Titus as a problem that even the Apostles were dealing with in that day and age:

> *"They profess that they know God; but in works they deny him, being abominable, and disobedient, and unto every good work reprobate."*[3]

---

[1]*Isaiah 24:6*

[2]*Matthew 7:19-24*

[3]*Titus 1:16*

While there is only one way to be saved, and Jesus Christ is that one and only way, we clearly must do more than just confess Jesus. We must show Him that we have truly taken His spirit into our hearts to be born anew. In other words, talk is often very cheap, and there are those who go about and will say and do many things to deceive. The true test to know if someone has taken Jesus as their personal Savior is by their *"fruits,"* because by their fruits we shall know them. As proof of the Lord Jesus in our hearts, our *"fruits in Lord Jesus,"* we must keep His commandments.

> ***"If ye love me, keep my commandments.***
>
> ***"He that hath my commandments, and keepeth them, he it is that loveth me: and he that loveth me shall be loved of my Father, and I will love him, and will manifest myself to him.***
>
> *"Judas saith unto him, not Iscariot, Lord, how is it that thou wilt manifest thyself unto us, and not unto the world?*
>
> ***"Jesus answered and said unto him, If a man love me, he will keep my words: and my Father will love him, and we will come unto him, and make our abode with him.***
>
> *" He that loveth me not keepeth not my sayings: and the word which ye hear is not mine, but the Father's which sent me."*[1]

> *"Abide in me, and I in you. As the branch cannot bear fruit of itself, except it abide in the vine; no more can ye, except ye abide in me.*
>
> ***"I am the vine, ye are the branches: He that abideth in me, and I in him, the same bringeth forth much fruit: for without me ye can do nothing.***
>
> *"If a man abide not in me, he is cast forth as a branch, and is withered; and men gather them, and cast them into the fire, and they are burned.*
>
> *"If ye abide in me, and my words abide in you, ye shall ask what ye will, and it shall be done unto you.*
>
> *"Herein is my Father glorified, that ye bear much fruit; so shall ye be my disciples.*
>
> *"As the Father hath loved me, so have I loved you: continue ye in my love.*
>
> *"If ye keep my commandments, ye shall abide in my love; even as*

---

[1] *John 14:15, 21-24*

107

I have kept my Father's commandments, and abide in his love."[1]

Beyond the ten commandments, which are contained in the two great commandments;

> *"Master, which is the great commandment in the law?*
> *"Jesus said unto him, Thou shalt love the Lord thy God with all thy heart, and with all thy soul, and with all thy mind.*
> *"This is the first and great commandment.*
> *"And the second is like unto it, Thou shalt love thy neighbour as thyself.*
> *"On these two commandments hang all the law and the prophets."* [2]

Peter listed some of the additional "fruits" that would come forth from those truly professing Jesus.

> *"Whereby are given unto us exceeding great and precious promises: that by these ye might be partakers of the divine nature, having escaped the corruption that is in the world through lust.*
> *"And beside this, giving all diligence, add to your **faith** virtue; and to **virtue** knowledge;*
> *"And to **knowledge** temperance; and to **temperance** patience; and to **patience** godliness;*
> *"And to **godliness** brotherly kindness; and to **brotherly kindness** charity.*
> *"For if these things be in you, and abound, they make you that ye shall neither be barren nor unfruitful in the knowledge of our Lord Jesus Christ.*
> *"But he that lacketh these things is blind, and cannot see afar off, and hath forgotten that he was purged from his old sins."* [3]

> *"But the fruit of the Spirit is love, joy, peace, longsuffering,*

---

[1] *John 15:4-10*

[2] *Matthew 22:36-40*

[3] *2 Peter 1:4-9*

gentleness, goodness, faith,
"Meekness, temperance:
"If we live in the Spirit, let us also walk in the Spirit." [1]

"And this is life eternal, that they might know thee the only true
God, and Jesus Christ, whom thou hast sent." [2]

Perhaps the best way to describe what I believe the Bible teaches us about truly coming to Jesus, is by relating a simple Sunday School story.

Three men died and went to heaven. An angel met them at the gates of judgement and indicated that before they received their appropriate mansion above or were sent elsewhere, they would have to have an interview. They were led down a hallway to a beautiful waiting room where they were told to sit, pending their call for their interview.

The first man was called and entered the room where he encountered a man seated behind a simple desk. In front of the man at the desk were several large books. The man motioned for him to sit down and then opened one of the books, taking a very brief minute to peruse something. He then looked up and asked the man what he knew about Jesus Christ.

The man responded by saying that he had read the Bible a little and had gone to church sometimes. He basically said that many said Jesus was the Son of God, and that He had died for our sins on a cross and taught people to be good. After a few minutes, when he had exhausted his knowledge of Jesus, he was excused and left by a side door.

The second man was then invited in and asked the same question, "What do you know about Jesus?" This time the man responded saying he was quite an authority about Jesus, having received three separate master's degrees from college, a doctorate, and having written several books on the subject. He then proceeded to go into much detail concerning the life and teachings of Jesus Christ. After a few hours of recitation, the interviewer kindly thanked the man and he also left by the side door.

---

[1] *Galatians 5:22, 23, 25*

[2] *John 17:3*

The third man was then invited into the room where he immediately fell to his knees, proclaiming, "Master." The person seated behind the desk then came around and stood before the man. It was when the interviewer raised him up to embrace him that the man noticed the marks from the nails in the feet and in the hands of the interviewer. "Welcome home, my good and faithful servant," said the Lord Jesus.

"I am the good shepherd, and know my sheep, and am known of mine."[1]

Those Who Will Not Rise to Heaven

The Bible is even more explicit concerning those who will not survive the last days and will be burned at the last day. Just a few quotes will suffice. Paul wrote:

"Now the works of the flesh are manifest, which are these; Adultery, fornication, uncleanness, lasciviousness,
"Idolatry, witchcraft, hatred, variance, emulations, wrath, strife, seditions, heresies,
"Envyings, murders, drunkenness, revellings, and such like: of the which I tell you before, as I have also told you in time past, that **they which do such things shall not inherit the kingdom of God."**[2]

Paul specifically wrote to Timothy telling him that in the last days these things would be rampant among men:

"This know also, that in the last days perilous times shall come.
"For men shall be lovers of their own selves, covetous, boasters, proud, blasphemers, disobedient to parents, unthankful, unholy,
"Without natural affection, trucebreakers, false accusers, incontinent, fierce, despisers of those that are good,
"Traitors, heady, highminded, lovers of pleasures more than lovers of God;
"Having a form of godliness, but denying the power thereof: from

---

[1]John 10:14

[2]Galatians 5:19-21

such turn away.

"For of this sort are they which creep into houses, and lead captive silly women laden with sins, led away with divers lusts,

"Ever learning, and never able to come to the knowledge of the truth.

"Now as Jannes and Jambres withstood Moses, so do these also resist the truth: men of corrupt minds, reprobate concerning the faith.

"But they shall proceed no further: for their folly shall be manifest unto all men, as theirs also was. "[1]

Thus ends the listing of events leading up to the Second Coming of the Lord Jesus. One of the problems associated with listing these events comes from the fact that there are often many things transpiring at the same time. I have tried to represent the events of the transition period between the 6th Seal and the 7th Seal in a visual way with the following timeline. It is my intention for readers to obtain a rough idea of the flow of events concerning this special period of time so that they can perhaps gain a better understanding of what is happening around us and perhaps make their own estimation of where we are in relation to these prophesied events. Some events and their appropriate time references are not mentioned specifically in the Bible. These I have marked with a ? and have placed them where I felt logically they might fit in.

It is my personal opinion that we are in the unknown period of time just prior to the start of the 6th Plague, the great world war that George Washington saw in vision.

---

[1] *2 Timothy 3:1-9*

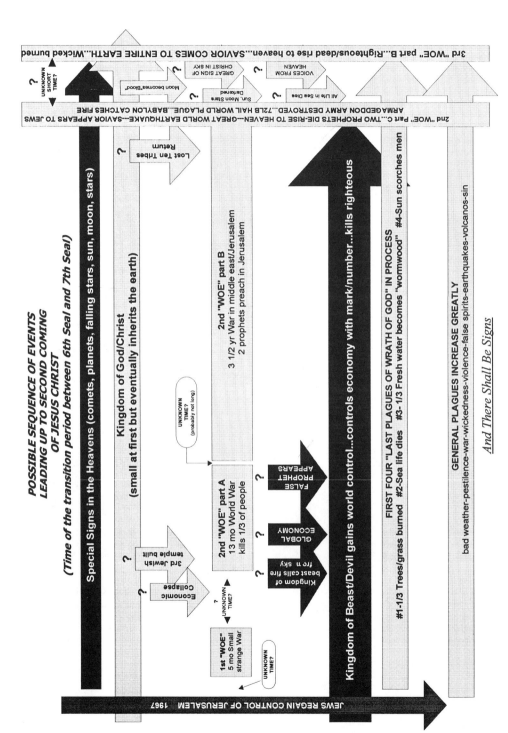

POSSIBLE SEQUENCE OF EVENTS
LEADING UP TO SECOND COMING
OF JESUS CHRIST

(Time of the transition period between 6th Seal and 7th Seal)

Special Signs in the Heavens (comets, planets, falling stars, sun, moon, stars)

Kingdom of God/Christ
(small at first but eventually inherits the earth)

3rd "WOE"..part B...Righteous/dead rise to heaven..."SAVIOR COMES TO ENTIRE EARTH"...Wicked burned

UNKNOWN SHORT TIME?

GREAT SIGN OF CHRIST IN SKY

Moon becomes"Blood"

Sun, Moon Stars Darkened

VOICES FROM HEAVEN

All Life in Sea Dies

2nd "WOE" Part C...TWO PROPHETS DIE-RISE TO HEAVEN—GREAT WORLD EARTHQUAKE—SAVIOR APPEARS TO JEWS
ARMAGEDDON ARMY DESTROYED...72LB HAIL WORLD PLAGUE...BABYLON CATCHES FIRE

Lost Ten Tribes Return

2nd "WOE" part B
3 1/2 yr War in middle east/Jerusalem
2 prophets preach in Jerusalem

3rd Jewish temple built

2nd "WOE" part A
13 mo World War
kills 1/3 of people

UNKNOWN TIME? (probably not long)

FALSE PROPHET APPEARS

GLOBAL ECONOMY

Kingdom of beast calls fire fro'm sky

Economic Collapse

UNKNOWN TIME?

1st "WOE"
5 mo Small strange War

UNKNOWN TIME?

Kingdom of Beast/Devil gains world control...controls economy with mark/number...kills righteous

FIRST FOUR "LAST PLAGUES OF WRATH OF GOD" IN PROCESS
#1-1/3 Trees/grass burned   #2-Sea life dies   #3- 1/3 Fresh water becomes "wormwood"   #4-Sun scorches men

GENERAL PLAGUES INCREASE GREATLY
bad weather-pestilence-war-wickedness-violence-false spirits-earthquakes-volcanos-sin

JEWS REGAIN CONTROL OF JERUSALEM   1967

And There Shall Be Signs

CHAPTER VI
AND NOW...THE GOOD NEWS

Escaping the Terrible Events of the Last Days

Often many who read and discuss the scriptures concerning the events of the last days, concentrate primarily upon the terrible events that have been prophesied. This is fairly easy to do because there are several terrible events that will happen in the near future. Even the Apostles of Christ had to be cautioned to not be terrified because of these events:

> *"But when ye shall hear of wars and commotions, be not terrified: for these things must first come to pass;"*[1]

Christ then went on to describe some more of the future events, and then He gave them these comforting words:

> *"And when these things begin to come to pass, then look up, and lift up your heads; for your redemption draweth nigh."*[2]

Often the Second Coming of Jesus Christ is called the end of the world. This is incorrect in that it is not the end of the world, but it is the end for murderers, liars, thieves, adulterers, fornicators, witches, sorcerers, etc. For those who do not fall into any of those categories, it is really just a difficult time of change to an unbelievably wonderful time, a time of peace and happiness which has never before been experienced on earth.

The Bible likens this period of change unto a woman giving birth....at first it is exciting to think that a baby is coming, then it changes to a long waiting, and then grows into uncomfortableness and difficulty with a great desire to get it over with. The time seems to go on forever. Will the day ever come? Each day is more uncomfortable and difficult, and enduring to the end takes on real meaning. Then quickly, often when least expecting it, it changes to real pain instead of

---

[1]*Luke 21:9*

[2]*Luke 21:28*

uncomfortableness. The relatively short pains of labor are real, very hard, excruciatingly painful, and are so difficult that if they weren't short, the mother-to-be would surely die. But, luckily, they are relatively short and *" as soon as she is delivered of the child, she remembereth no more the anguish, for joy that a man is born into the world."* (John 16:21)

There are so many parallels between the birth process and the Second Coming. The good news is that the majority of the righteous will survive the extremely difficult times ahead, passing through them... while we know for a surety that the wicked will not. If we are prepared for those things which are coming, both spiritually and physically, then we stand a pretty good chance to avoid the most dire consequences of some, if not all of these events. The Savior himself said:

> *"Watch ye therefore, and pray always, that ye may be accounted worthy to escape all these things that shall come to pass,"* [1]

In Joel, as he describes the final wars of Armageddon, he indicates the very same thing:

> *"And it shall come to pass, that whosoever shall call on the name of the Lord shall be delivered: for in mount Zion and in Jerusalem shall be deliverance, as the Lord hath said, and in the remnant whom the Lord shall call."* [2]

Besides what is recorded in Luke and Joel, in Matthew, there is a whole chapter about those righteous who survive the events of the last days. In each of these parables (the parable of the ten virgins, the talents, the sheep and goats, as well as in Matt 24:37-51 the verses talking about life continuing on with eating and marriage, two in the field, two grinding, and the faithful and wise servant, also the parable of the wheat and tares in Matt 13:24-30), there are both righteous and wicked who have survived most of the terrible plagues. At the very end, when the great sign of the Son of Man shows forth, the righteous are lifted away from the earth and the remaining wicked receive the final recompense of their evil actions. True, the Bible indicates that there will be much less righteous than wicked, but those few will be there at the very end and will return to the earth to inherit it. The Savior calls them the *"meek."*

---

[1] *Luke 21:36*

[2] *Joel 2:32*

"Blessed are the meek: for they shall inherit the earth." [1]

The Bible dictionary describes meek as gentle, forgiving, benevolent and humble. These are those that will survive the events (the cleansing of the wheat field of the tares) of the last days.

And so it is again a case of, 'is the glass half full or half empty?' A lot of this would depend again on a person's own personal outlook and spiritual preparation... are we the peaceable followers of Christ, or are we the servants of the evil one? Each day we have to make that decision to follow one or the other. Joshua and Jesus said:

> *"...choose you this day whom ye will serve; whether the gods which your fathers served that were on the other side of the flood, or the gods of the Amorites, in whose land ye dwell: but as for me and my house, we will serve the LORD."*[2]

> *"No man can serve two masters: for either he will hate the one, and love the other; or else he will hold to the one, and despise the other. Ye cannot serve God and mammon."*[3]

Besides the direct Biblical references mentioned above that indicate that the majority of the righteous will survive the events of the last days, there are biblical/ historical precedences as well. Time after time the Bible records that when a majority of people in a given town/city, country, region or even the world choose wickedness over righteousness, then the consequences of those actions do come upon them and the righteous do suffer. However, in almost every instance we have record of, the majority of the righteous escape the more part of the terrible consequences.

We could go into some detail about Enoch and his city, Noah and the flood, Sodom and Gomorrah and others... but suffice it to be said that in every case the righteous, though few in numbers, persecuted and passing through difficult times, were faithful and survived the destruction of their wicked neighbors.

---

[1] Matt 5:5

[2] Joshua 24:15

[3] Matthew 6:24

A very interesting experience is recorded by Ezekiel concerning the first destruction of Jerusalem, which has some parallels in what John records concerning the last days. Just before the Lord destroyed Jerusalem (the first Abomination of Desolation wherein Jerusalem was sieged, looted and then destroyed by fire with 2/3 of the inhabitants of Israel perishing), he gave Ezekiel a vision in which he sent an angel to put a mark in the forehead of the righteous. Those not so marked were destroyed, including old and young, women, and men.

> *"And the Lord said unto him, Go through the midst of the city, through the midst of Jerusalem, and **set a mark upon the foreheads of the men that sigh and that cry for all the abominations that be done in the midst thereof.***
>
> *"And to the others he said in mine hearing, Go ye after him through the city, and smite: let not your eye spare, neither have ye pity:*
>
> *"Slay utterly old and young, both maids, and little children, and women: but come not near any man upon whom is the mark; and begin at my sanctuary.*
>
> *"...and they went forth, and slew in the city."*[1]

We have a little record of some of the righteous that escaped death, but went into captivity, including Daniel.

Importantly, John in his Revelation sees something very similar for the righteous in the last days:

> *"And I saw another angel ascending from the east, having the seal of the living God: and he cried with a loud voice to the four angels, to whom it was given to hurt the earth and the sea,*
>
> *"Saying, Hurt not the earth, neither the sea, nor the trees,**till we have sealed the servants of our God in their foreheads."***
>
> *"And I heard the number of them which were sealed: and there were sealed an hundred and forty and four thousand of all the tribes of the children of Israel.*

---

[1] *Ezekiel 9:4-7*

> *"After this I beheld, and, lo, a great multitude, which no man could number, of all nations, and kindreds, and people, and tongues,.. "*[1]

John, in his Revelation, similarly to Ezekiel, also sees an angel marking the forehead of the righteous, specifically an initial group of 144,000 and then later a *"great multitude which no man could number."* Also in Rev 22:4, John specifically sees those who pass through this cleansing of the earth and inherit the earth (the meek) are those who have had the name of Christ *"in their foreheads:"*

Conversely, John also describes the devil doing the same thing to those that serve him. Besides possibly referring to a physical mark needed, along with a number or name, the mark of the beast is probably referring in the same way as the spiritual mark of God, because later John is informed that it is those who worship the beast and his image and receive the mark of his name that will drink of the wrath of God.

> *"And the third angel followed them, saying with a loud voice, If any man worship the beast and his image, and receive his mark in his forehead, or in his hand,*
> *"The same shall drink of the wine of the wrath of God, which is poured out without mixture into the cup of his indignation:..*
> *"And the smoke of their torment ascendeth up for ever and ever: and they have no rest day nor night, who worship the beast and his image, and whosoever receiveth the mark of his name"*[2]

This marking of the forehead is something that has great symbolism throughout the Bible, denoting the righteous from the wicked. John describes a wicked kingdom, spiritual or physical we are not certain, with a title on her forehead:

> *"And upon her forehead was a name written, MYSTERY, BABYLON THE GREAT, THE MOTHER OF HARLOTS AND ABOMINATIONS OF THE EARTH."* [3]

---

[1] *Rev 7:2-4, 9*

[2] Revelation 14:9-12

[3] *Revelation 17:5*

For example, Moses was told by God to literally put just the opposite title upon Aaron's forehead:

> *"And thou shalt make a plate of pure gold, and grave upon it, like the engravings of a signet,* **HOLINESS TO THE LORD**.
>
> *"And thou shalt put it on a blue lace, that it may be upon the mitre; upon the forefront of the mitre it shall be.*
>
> *"**And it shall be upon Aaron's forehead**, that Aaron may bear the iniquity of the holy things, which the children of Israel shall hallow in all their holy gifts; **and it shall be always upon his forehead, that they may be accepted before the LORD**."*[1]

And so in conclusion, though the Lord doesn't specifically mention in the Bible exactly how He will spare the righteous, time after time after time He does directly say that He will spare the majority of the righteous the terrible consequences of the wicked majority. John says that in the last days some of the righteous will die, just as this tragedy happens from time to time in daily life throughout the history of the earth, but that their death would be unto the Lord.

> *"And I heard a voice from heaven saying unto me, Write, Blessed are the dead which die in the Lord from henceforth: Yea, saith the Spirit, that they may rest from their labours; and their works do follow them."*[2]

The real message and hope brought by John and the other prophets recording their visions/foreknowledge for us to read in the Bible, is this: by remaining true to the commandments of God, and the faith of Jesus, we will rise to meet Him and then return with Him to live on earth during a time of incredible peace and happiness.

> *"Here is the patience of the saints: here are they that keep the commandments of God, and the faith of Jesus."*
>
> *"And I saw a new heaven and a new earth: for the first heaven and the first earth were passed away; and there was no more sea.*
>
> *"And I John saw the holy city, new Jerusalem, coming down from God out of heaven, prepared as a bride adorned for her husband.*

---

[1] *Exodus 28:36-38*

[2] *Rev 14:13*

"And I heard a great voice out of heaven saying, Behold, the tabernacle of God is with men, and he will dwell with them, and they shall be his people, and God himself shall be with them, and be their God

"And God shall wipe away all tears from their eyes; and there shall be no more death, neither sorrow, nor crying, neither shall there be any more pain: for the former things are passed away.[1]

---

[1]*Rev 14:12, 21:1-4*

CHAPTER VII

CONCLUSION/SUMMARY

There are three points that I wish to bring out.

First, the signs as prophesied in the Old and New Testament, clearly indicate that the Second Coming of Jesus Christ is very near. The weather will continue to become worse, more violent and unpredictable, along with a continued increase in other disasters such as droughts, floods, tornados, diseases, famines, pestilences, earthquakes, volcanoes, etc. Life and nature as we have known it during the previous millennium will change. Wickedness and evil will continue to grow in all of its many forms... suicides, murders, wars, violence, abuse, lyings, deceivings, false Christs, family breakups, witchcrafts, false spiritualism, perversions, homosexuality, adultery, lust, greed, etc. will continually fill the news. Preparations need to be made, both physically and spiritually.

Second, in my opinion, the signs indicate that we are probably just before the start of the Sixth Plague, the thirteen month war that will kill 1/3 of the people on earth with nuclear and biological weapons. This world war will affect all nations, but according to George Washington, it will be especially severe in the United States. Soon after this war, another war will begin which is often called the "Battle of Armageddon," and will center in the Middle East, involving all of the nations of the earth. It is near the end of this 3 ½ year war that the worldwide earthquake happens, signaling the imminent return of the Savior.

Why will this 13 month war be so devastating in the United States? Because this nation was founded as a Christian nation, and, having at one time been so blessed with the knowledge of the gospel of Jesus, too many people of this nation have rejected Him as their Savior, choosing instead to follow other gods of lust, wealth, power, perversion, self indulgence and pride. The consequences of such actions are about to come upon this nation in full force.

A historical observation/quote helps summarize the current situation facing the world, but primarily the United States, as outlined in the Bible:

"History fails to record a single precedent in which nations subject to moral decay have not passed into political and economic decline.

"There has either been a spiritual awakening to overcome the moral lapse, or a progressive deterioration leading to ultimate national disaster."[1]

On a scriptural basis, as one studies the Old Testament, there seems to be three major moral breakdowns, or sins, that seem to always prelude the imminent destruction of a society, or nation. For the most part, they seem to always appear together and are often mentioned as somewhat the "last straws" as the prophets of God warn the society of impending destruction. The first is specifically directed at those societies that were founded or based upon God's laws.

1. Keeping the Sabbath day holy. (It doesn't seem to matter what day it is, as long as there is a day kept to honor and reverence God.)

2. The neglect, persecution, ill treatment and murder of the poor, sick, needy and the widows.

3. The embrace of degenerate moral practices, with homosexuality leading the list.

Other peculiar "sins" seemingly accompany these three and are often mentioned as well, including sorceries, witchcrafts, enchantments, familiar spirits (See Chronicles 33:6, Isa 47:9-12) and sometimes even human sacrifice. (Sorceries, fornication, murder, thefts and idle worship are mentioned as specific sins that the world in the last days does not repent of even after the 13 month world war. See Revelation 9:20-21. An extremely troubling question, also to be considered is, "In the eyes of God, what is the difference between sacrificing children to idols, and sacrificing children (abortion) to the modern day idol of selfishness?")

As mentioned before, Paul seemed to have special insight as to the moral condition of the world just prior to the Savior's Second Coming. In his second letter to Timothy he wrote:

"This know also, that in the last days perilous times shall come.

---

[1]*General Douglas McArthur*

121

"For men shall be lovers of their own selves, covetous, boasters, proud, blasphemers, disobedient to parents, unthankful, unholy,

"Without natural affection, trucebreakers, false accusers, incontinent, fierce, despisers of those that are good,

"Traitors, heady, highminded, lovers of pleasures more than lovers of God:

"Having a form of godliness, but denying the power thereof: from such turn away.

"But evil men and seducers shall wax worse and worse, deceiving, and being deceived." [1]

Paul reminds us often that the kingdom of God is not made up of those who commit such sins as:

"...Adultery, fornication, uncleanness, lascivisouness,

"Idolatry, witchcraft, hatred, variance, emulations, wrath, strife, seditions, heresies,

"Envyings, murders, drunkenness, revellings and such like..."
"...Shall not inherit the kingdom of God." [2]

He, as well as others, often mentioned that there will be false spiritual leaders in the last days, to be aware of them and avoid them at all costs. How will we be able to discern between the good and the evil among us, especially when the evil can be so cleverly disguised? The Savior very clearly told us a way to know false spiritual leaders from true spiritual leaders:

"Beware of false prophets, which come to you in sheep's clothing, but inwardly they are ravening wolves.

***"Ye shall know them by their fruits.** Do men gather grapes of thorns, or figs of thistles?*

"Even so every good tree bringeth forth good fruit; but a corrupt tree bringeth forth evil fruit." [3]

---

[1] *2 Tim 3:1-5,13*

[2] *Gal 5:19-21*

[3] *Matt 7:15-17*

What kinds of fruits help us to tell good men from evil men? Paul describes them as honest, true, chaste, and especially charitable....they don't keep company with fornicators and drunkards, and even abstain from all appearance of evil. We should look for and cultivate friends such as these.

James mentions that:

> *"Pure religion and undefiled before God and the Father is this, To visit the fatherless and widows in their affliction, and to keep himself unspotted from the world."[1]*

Too often we don't want to become involved in the fight for good and that which is right because by so doing we invite the attack of those*"who call evil good and good evil."* We should remember that those who follow Jesus, especially in the last days, will come under attack and persecution. We are commanded to not be weary in doing good (*Gal 6:9*), and Paul continually reminds us that it is a long race and we need to endure to the end. James said,*"Therefore to him that knoweth to do good, and doeth it not, to him it is sin."[2]* The Savior commanded us not to hide our candle under a bushel but instead to hold our candle high so that it would give light to those around us. The consequences of inaction are summed up simply:

**"Evil will always triumph when too many good men
stand by and do nothing"**

The sad trouble is that all of the aforementioned sins that seem to indicate the imminent destruction of a society (failure to keep Sabbath day holy, neglect of the poor, embrace of homosexuality, sorceries, witchcrafts, abortion, etc.) are extremely prevalent in our United States society and are growing. One only has to read the daily newspaper to see such filth and its natural consequences. Though much could be written upon these subjects, one quick example will serve as an adequate demonstration.

---

[1]*James 1:27*

[2]*James 4:17*

What the scriptures have to say about the 'Mother Earth is God" or the "GAIA" movement and homosexuality

Though centuries pass and technology advances, still, the Bible helps us to understand that throughout the ages the general problems and human nature of people remain essentially the same. This is both comforting and frightening at the same time. A perfect example of this is found in a growing movement that has become extremely powerful, to the point of changing the laws of nations to reflect their beliefs. This movement is called the 'GAIA' or 'Mother Earth' movement and is undoubtedly part of the evil 'kingdom of the beast' which has been foretold will come to control most of the world. Essentially it is a philosophy that teaches that the earth or nature is God, and that man is equal to or actually less than the animals and plants that inhabit the earth. This philosophy is anti-christ, denying the true and living God and His Son Jesus Christ.

Again, this philosophy is not new. Even in the days of the Apostles, they had those that taught that the world and nature was to be worshipped or was even god. Paul tells about this group of people who;

> *"...became vain in their imaginations, and their foolish heart was darkened.*
> *"Professing themselves to be wise, they became fools,*
> *"And changed the glory of the uncorruptible God into an image made like to corruptible man, and to birds, and fourfooted beasts, and creeping things.*
> *"Who changed the truth of God into a lie, and worshipped and served the creature more than the Creator..."[1]*

Continuing on, Paul tells us a very interesting thing about this group of 'Nature is God' or 'Mother Earth' people, in that they were primarily comprised of homosexuals and lesbians even in his day and age.

> *"For this cause God gave them up unto vile affections: for even their women did change the natural use into that which is against nature:*

---

[1]*Romans 1:21-23,25*

"And likewise also the men, leaving the natural use of the woman, burned in their lust one toward another; men with men working that which is unseemly..."[1]

Paul further describes this group of people as full of other sins as well;

"And even as they did not like to retain God in their knowledge, God gave them over to a reprobate mind, to do those things which are not convenient;

"Being filled with all unrighteousness, fornication, wickedness, covetousness, maliciousness; full of envy, murder, debate, deceit, malignity; whisperers,

"Backbiters, haters of God, despiteful, proud, boasters, inventors of evil things, disobedient to parents,

"Without understanding, covenantbreakers, without natural affection, implacable, unmerciful:

"Who knowing the judgement of God, that they which commit such things are worthy of death, not only do the same, but have pleasure in them that do them."[2]

It is very interesting to note that today in 'modern' times, the nucleus of the "mother earth is god" movement is again primarily composed of people that Paul so perfectly described in his day and age... homosexuals, lesbians, and other wicked people *"full of envy, covetousness, maliciousness, debate, deceit, malignity, haters of God, despiteful, boasters, unmerciful, inventors of evil things, proud,"* etc.

While the Savior taught that we should respect the plants, animals and the earth, in no way should we worship them as god or gods. The commandments are very specific on this point:

"Thou shalt have no other gods before me.

"Thou shalt not make unto thee any graven image, or any likeness of any thing that is in heaven above, or that is in the earth beneath, or that is in the water under the earth.

---

[1]*Romans 1:26-27*

[2]*Romans 1:28-32*

"Thou shalt not bow down thyself to them, nor serve them:[1]

The scriptures teach that plants and animals were placed here for man to watch over and care for while at the same time mankind was to *"have dominion over the fish of the sea, and over the fowl of the air, and over every living thing that moveth upon the earth."*[2]

Again, we are warned that in the last days anti-Christ teachings would flourish to the point of even deceiving the faithful. The adversary of all righteousness could and would easily subvert some good ideas and transform them into programs to lead people away from coming to Jesus. It is interesting to note that almost two thousand years ago the Apostles wrote of the kinds of beliefs and programs of those who embrace sin and wickedness, especially the perversions of homosexuality and lesbianism. Again, we are seeing it increase today... first it was an increase in perversion, and then the promotion of anti-christ/mother earth teachings. The appearance and strength of such anti-christ philosophies indicates the nearness of the consequences of such actions, ie, the destruction of the societies who embrace such evil practices.

Finally, it needs to be pointed out one last time, that for those who take Jesus as their personal Savior and follow His commandments... those who watch for the signs, pray always, keep His commandments and prepare themselves both spiritually and physically... will be able to avoid most of the terrible effects of the forthcoming judgements of God upon this wicked nation and the world. The promises have been made and His *"words shall not pass away."*

In conclusion, again, all that I am doing is adding my voice to the growing chorus that is shouting the warning to prepare ourselves both spiritually and physically for the Coming of our Lord and Savior, Jesus Christ. My hope and prayer is that some of the material contained herein might strike a responsive chord in a few individuals and families and cause them to take stock of their situation and possibly re-order their priorities, if needed, both by coming unto our Lord Jesus and by beginning some physical preparations for the hard times ahead.

---

[1]*Exodus 20:3-5*

[2]*See Gen 1:28-31*

May we all heed the words of Christ and come unto Him, taking upon us His name, keeping His commandments and follow His example so that we *"may be accounted worthy to escape all these things that shall come to pass, and to stand before the Son of man."*

"Watch therefore: for ye know not what hour your Lord doth come.

"Therefore be ye also ready: for in such an hour as ye think not the Son of man cometh.

"Blessed is that servant, whom his lord when he cometh shall find so doing." [1]

---

[1] Matt 24:42,44,46

APPENDIX
OF SUPPLEMENTAL
REFERENCES

LOOKING AT SCRIPTURES FROM DANIEL

Daniel's Second Vision

While in the third year of the reign of Belshazzar, in Daniel's second vision, he first sees himself at Shushan, the Persian capital, and then at the nearby river of Ulai. He then again sees kingdoms of the future in the form of a Ram and a H-Goat. Luckily, Daniel asks for an interpretation and Gabriel fills him in on some of the details. Again, it starts off with a kingdom he is familiar with and then goes on in the future, covering some of the same material as his prior dream, but giving some important detail not recorded before.

1. The Ram is the kings of Media and Persia represented by the two horns. (Daniel 8:3-4,20)

2. The Goat is the king of Greece with the horn as the first king. (Again, probably Alexander the Great.) (Daniel 8:5-8, 21)

3. Again, this kingdom is divided up into four kingdoms. (As mentioned before the kingdom of Greece was divided up between the four generals of Alexander, Ptolemy (Egypt), Selecus (Syria), Lysimachus (Thrace), and Cassander (Macedonia). (Daniel 8:8,22)

4. Next, *"a king of fierce countenance"* comes forth from these four kings and *"waxes great towards the south, east and pleasant land..."* *"but not by his own power,"* who destroys *"the mighty and the holy people,"* and takes away the daily sacrifice from the temple, and desolates the temple for 2300 days (6.3 years) when the temple will be cleansed. Eventually he dies without being killed, *"shall be broken without hand."*(Daniel 8:9-14, 23-25)

This is often interpreted to be Antiochus IV Epiphanes who ruled Palestine from 175-164 B.C, coming from Syria, because so much of the prophecy fits him so well. History records that he plundered and desecrated the Jewish temple (even sacrificed a pig to an image of Zeus on the temple altar), destroyed the walls of Jerusalem, sold tens of thousands of Jews as slaves, and murdered anyone who professed to be a Jew or observed a Jewish holiday.

Ruling from Syria, his rule over Israel was eventually overthrown by

Judas Maccabeus who then cleansed the temple. Interestingly enough, from the time that he killed the Jewish High Priest Onias III (172 B.C.), and began looting Palestine/Jerusalem/Temple, to the time of his defeat and death (164 B.C.), was a period of approximately 6+ years. Also, history records that when the news of his army's defeat reached him, he quickly died of a sudden illness.

Daniel's Third Vision

In Daniel's third vision which he received under the rule of Darius in Persia (having prophesied earlier of his removal to Persia after the defeat of the Babylonians), he had been praying to the Lord for forgiveness on behalf of his people and Jerusalem. The angel Gabriel then appears and gives him the answers he seeks, specifically giving Daniel a timetable of important events in the future.

1. Daniel is given to understand that seventy weeks/years of captivity of his people were almost up. (Daniel 9:24)

> *"Seventy weeks are determined upon thy people and upon thy holy city, to finish the transgression, and to make an end of sins, and to make reconciliation for iniquity, and to bring in everlasting righteousness, and to seal up the vision and prophecy, and to anoint the most holy."*

This occurred from the destruction of Jerusalem in 606 B.C. to the rebuilding of Jerusalem in 536 B.C.

2. The temple/Jerusalem would be rebuilt during troublesome times and then 69 weeks of 7 weeks (often interpreted as 69 years times 7 years or 7x69=483 years) from the command to rebuild the temple the Messiah would come. (Daniel 9:25)

> *"Know therefore and understand, that from the going forth of the commandment to restore and to build Jerusalem unto the Messiah the Prince shall be seven weeks, and threescore and two weeks: the street shall be built again, and the wall, even in troublous times."*

The decree to Ezra to rebuild the temple (See Ezra chapter 7) and which initiated the building of it, was given in 457 B.C. by Darius (An earlier decree had been given by Cyrus but not carried out), and was undertaken with problems (*"troubled them in building"*) caused by the Samaritans. (see Ezra 4:4)   Interestingly enough, from 457 B.C. it was 483 years to 26 A.D., which is observed as the traditional day that Jesus began His public ministry.

3. The Messiah *"shall confirm the covenant with many for one week: and in the midst of the week he shall cause the sacrifice and the oblation to cease,"*

> *"And he shall confirm the covenant with many for one week: and in the midst of the week he shall cause the sacrifice and the oblation to cease, and for the overspreading of abominations he shall make it desolate, even until the consumation, and that determined shall be poured upon the desolate."* (Daniel 9:27)

The Messiah/Christ was crucified after 3 ½ years or *"in the midst"* of a 7 year week. His death/sacrifice ceased the sacrifice of the shedding of animals (see Heb chapter 10) and in its place instituted the sacrament of his flesh and blood. Because of His death by the Jews, the temple and Jerusalem would once again be made desolate.

4. After 62 weeks the Messiah shall be cut off and Jerusalem and the temple shall be destroyed with much war and desolations.

> *"And after threescore and two weeks shall Messiah be cut off, but not for himself: and the people of the prince that shall come shall destroy the city and the sanctuary; and the end thereof shall be with a flood, and unto the end of the war desolations are determined." (Daniel 9:26)*

The Romans under Titus destroyed Jerusalem and the temple (as Christ himself prophesied in Luke 21:), in 70 A.D.

Daniel's Fourth Vision

In Daniel's fourth vision, he receives an angelic visitor who proclaims:

> *"Now I am come to make thee understand what shall befall thy people in the latter days: for yet the vision is for many days."* (Daniel 10:14)

What is meant by the latter days is not entirely clear. By analyzing the wars back and forth as described in the vision, and then relating them to historical events, most bibilical scholars seem to agree upon the following as being what is described. Basically, it describes the period of time from Daniel to the time just prior to the birth of Jesus Christ.

1. Three kings yet in Persia and the fourth king of Persia would be the greatest yet.

> *"And now will I shew thee the truth. Behold, there shall stand up yet three kings in Persia; and the fourth shall be far richer than they all: and by his strength through his riches he shall stir up all against the realm of Grecia."* (Daniel 11:2)

The four kings of Persia were Cyrus, Cambyses II, Darius, and Xerxes. Xerxes invaded Greece in 480 B.C. but was defeated at Salamia.

2. Another mighty king would come forth and rule with great dominion and his kingdom divided into four kingdoms.

> *"And a mighty king shall stand up, that shall rule with great dominion, and do according to his will.*
> *"And when he shall stand up, his kingdom shall be broken, and shall be divided toward the four winds of heaven; and not to his posterity, nor according to his dominion which he ruled: for his kingdom shall be plucked up, even for others beside those."* (Daniel 11:3-4)

Again, a reference to Alexander the Great/Greece and the kingdom being divided among his four generals.

3. The king of the South shall be strong and one of his princes shall be strong above him.

The king of the south was Ptolemy who ruled over Egypt. Seleucus helped Ptolemy defeat Antigonus in 325 B.C. and then became the master of Mesopotamia and Syria, to the North of Egypt.

4. The South king and his prince will join together for the South king's daughter will join with a king of the North. However, she will not retain strength, nor will the king of the north *"stand."*

Years later, they joined forces after Ptolemy II's daughter, Berenice, married Antiochus II of Syria. Antiochus II divorced his wife, Laodice, to marry Berenice. Later, Laodice had Antiochus II, Berenice and their son murdered.

5. Out of the South king's daughters roots will a king come with an army and prevail against the king of the North and bring captives and plunder back to Egypt.

Ptolemy III, Berenice's brother, defeated the son of Laodice, Seleucus II and did indeed bring slaves and plunder back to Egypt.

6. The sons of the North king shall gather forces and one should *"pass through"* and return to his fortress. The South king would attack the North king with a great multitude, but despite the great army, the South King will lose. Later the North King will go against the South King with much riches and a large army and take Egypt.

War waged back and forth until finally Antiochus III, son of Seleucus II (North King) finally defeated the Egyptians in 201 B.C. in Gaza when the Egyptians (South King) came north with a great army. Later, in 199 B.C., Antiochus III went south and conquered the Egyptians at Banias.

7. The North King shall wage war against the "isle" and shall win against many, but not all and eventually return to Syria. A raiser of taxes would succeed him, but would be shortly destroyed *"neither in anger nor in battle."*

Antiochus III turned his attention against Greece and Pergamon but the Romans defeated him in 190 B.C. He returned broke to Syria where he died in 187 B.C. Selecus IV came to the throne and sent out a tax collector to refill the treasury, but the tax collector, Heliodorus, assassinated the king after he was ordered to loot the Jewish temple.

8. A vile person shall come in and take the kingdom peaceably by flatteries. This vile person will slay the prince of the covenant and shall conquer, take much prey and spoil against the covenant people. He will go against the King of the South with a great army and shall conquer and loot. He will come again against the South but will not be successful because the ships of Chittim (Cyprus) shall come against him. He turns his wrath against the holy covenant, shall take away the daily sacrifice, and shall place the abomination that maketh desolate.

As mentioned before, an extremely vile king came into power illegally in Syria, Antiochus IV Epiphanes. He conquered Palestine, killed the Jewish High Priest Onias III and looted everywhere. He conquered and looted Egypt in 169 B.C., but when he went again against Egypt he was prevented by the Romans, primarily being defeated in naval battles. Antiochus IV, desecrated the Jewish temple, took away the daily sacrifices and devastated Jerusalem.

9. The people who know God will be strong but will fall by the sword and by flame for many days. The vile king of the North will do according to his will, will magnify himself above every god and shall prosper until his time is over. A strange god will he honor, which his fathers knew not, a god of forces.

The Jews mounted a revolt against Antiochus IV (called the Maccabean wars), eventually defeating his armies after over 30 years of rebellion. Antiochus called himself Epiphanes which means "god manifest" and substituted the god Zeus for the god Apollo, which had been the chief god of the Syrians/Seleucids before him.

10. At *"the time of the end"* the South King will come against the North king, be defeated, and the North King will loot Egypt and many countries, including *"the glorious land,"* but then will come back to the North because of troubles, *"plant the tabernacles of his palace between the seas*

in the glorious holy mountain," **and eventually come to his end.**

These last few verses seem to be a recap of the end of Antiochus IV Epiphanes.

A. Antiochus IV came into power around 175 B.C. Ptolemy Philometor tried to expand Egypt *("push"?)* after the death of Cleopatra around 173 B.C. Antiochus IV had begun looting Palestine about this time and had deposed (and later killed) the Jewish High Priest Onias III, whom Antiochus IV replaced with a new High Priest, Jason. (Daniel 11:40)

B. With a great army, Antiochus went south, conquering almost all countries in his path and defeated the Egpytians in 170 B.C. He then looted Egypt and returned home. In 169 B.C., with an even larger army, Antiochus invades Egypt a second time, but is thwarted by the Romans under Gaices Popilius Laenas. (Daniel 11:41-43)

C. About this same time Jason seizes Jerusalem *("tidings out of the east and out of the north shall trouble him" could easily refer to Rome and Jerusalem?*) and then on his return to the North, Antiochus savagely attacks and loots Jerusalem (Abomination of desecration), desecrating the temple (placing his standards and idols all over Jerusalem and the temple, even to the point of sacrificing a pig to his god Zeus upon the altar in the temple--- which perhaps corresponds to the verse *"And he shall plant the tabernacles of his palace between the seas in the glorious holy mountain;"*), killing tens of thousands of Jews and carrying away thousands of others into captivity. (Daniel 11:44)

D. An old Jewish priest, Matathias, began the revolt and his son Judas Maccabeus eventually defeated Antiochus IV, which led quickly to his death. (Daniel 11:45)

THE PROPHET JOEL'S DESCRIPTION OF THE ARMAGEDDON ARMY ATTACKING JERUSALEM/ISRAEL

The prophet Joel (in Joel Chapters 1,2 and 3), provides two brief descriptions of the terrible Armageddon army that attacks Jerusalem and is eventually destroyed. There are many parallels between this account and the account described in Daniel.

Joel describes a tremendous army, "*a great people and a strong; there hath not been ever the like, neither shall be any more after it, even to the years of many generations,*" that destroys everything in its path which descends upon and eventually overruns Jerusalem "*They shall run to and fro in the city; they shall run upon the wall, they shall climb up upon the houses; they shall enter in at the windows like a thief.*" This army comes apparently from the North, but because of the prayers by the elders, priests and the congregation, the army is eventually driven off "*into a land barren and desolate, with his face toward the east sea, and his hinder part toward the utmost sea,*" where it is eventually destroyed. "*and his stink shall come up, and his ill savor shall come up, because he hath done great things.*" Those who survive this terrible army are blessed with the millennial blessings of prosperity, rain, full harvests, etc.

Here are the actual scriptural references summarized above:

> "*For a nation is come up upon my land, strong, and without number, whose teeth are the teeth of a lion, and he hath the cheek teeth of a great lion.*
>
> "*The meat offering and the drink offering is cut off from the house of the Lord; the priests, the Lord's ministers, mourn.*
>
> "*How do the beasts groan! the herds of cattle are perplexed, because they have no pasture; yea, the flocks of sheep are made desolate.*
>
> "*O Lord, to thee will I cry: for the fire hath devoured the pastures of the wilderness, and the flame hath burned all the trees of the field.*
>
> "*The beasts of the field cry also unto thee: for the rivers of waters are dried up, and the fire hath devoured the pastures of the wilderness.*"

"Blow ye the trumpet in Zion, and sound an alarm in my holy mountain: let all the inhabitants of the land tremble: for the day of the Lord cometh, for it is nigh at hand

"A day of darkness and of gloominess, a day of clouds and of thick darkness, as the morning spread upon the mountains: a great people and a strong; there hath not been ever the like, neither shall be any more after it, even to the years of many generations.

"A fire devoureth before them; and behind them a flame burneth: the land is as the garden of Eden before them, and behind them a desolate wilderness; yea, and nothing shall escape them.

"The appearance of them is as the appearance of horses; and as horsemen, so shall they run.

"Like the noise of chariots on the tops of mountains shall they leap, like the noise of a flame of fire that devoureth the stubble, as a strong people set in battle array.

"Before their face the people shall be much pained: all faces shall gather blackness.

"They shall run like mighty men; they shall climb the wall like men of war; and they shall march every one on his ways, and they shall not break their ranks:

"Neither shall one thrust one another; they shall walk every one in his path: and when they fall upon the sword, they shall not be wounded.

"They shall run to and fro in the city; they shall run upon the wall, they shall climb up upon the houses; they shall enter in at the windows like a thief.

"The earth shall quake before them; the heavens shall tremble: the sun and the moon shall be dark, and the stars shall withdraw their shining.

Joel 2:11

"And the Lord shall utter his voice before his army: for his camp is very great: for he is strong that executeth his word: for the day of the Lord is great and very terrible; and who can abide it?

"Therefore also now, saith the Lord, turn ye even to me with all your heart, and with fasting, and with weeping, and with mourning:

"And rend your heart, and not your garments, and turn unto the Lord your God: for he is gracious and merciful, slow to anger, and of great kindness, and repenteth him of the evil.

"Blow the trumpet in Zion, sanctify a fast, call a solemn assembly:

"Gather the people, sanctify the congregation, assemble the elders, gather the children, and those that suck the breasts: let the bridegroom go forth of his chamber, and the bride out of her closet.

"Let the priests, the ministers of the Lord, weep between the porch and the altar, and let them say, Spare thy people, O Lord, and give not thine heritage to reproach, that the heathen should rule over them: wherefore should they say among the people, Where is their God?

"Then will the Lord be jealous for his land, and pity his people.

"Yea, the Lord will answer and say unto his people, Behold, I will send you corn, and wine, and oil, and ye shall be satisfied therewith: and I will no more make you a reproach among the heathen:

Joel 2:20

"But I will remove far off from you the northern army, and will drive him into a land barren and desolate, with his face toward the east sea, and his hinder part toward the utmost sea, and his stink shall come up, and his ill savor shall come up, because he hath done great things.

"Fear not, O land; be glad and rejoice: for the Lord will do great things.

"Be not afraid, ye beasts of the field: for the pastures of the wilderness do spring, for the tree beareth her fruit, the fig tree and the vine do yield their strength.

"Be glad then, ye children of Zion, and rejoice in the Lord your God: for he hath given you the former rain moderately, and he will cause to come down for you the rain, the former rain, and the latter rain in the first month.

"And the floors shall be full of wheat, and the fats shall overflow with wine and oil.

"And I will restore to you the years that the locust hath eaten, the cankerworm, and the caterpillar, and the palmerworm, my great army which I sent among you.

"And ye shall eat in plenty, and be satisfied, and praise the name of the Lord your God, that hath dealt wondrously with you: and my people shall never be ashamed.

"And ye shall know that I am in the midst of Israel, and that I am the Lord your God, and none else: and my people shall never be ashamed.

"And it shall come to pass afterward, that I will pour out my spirit upon all flesh; and your sons and your daughters shall prophesy, your old men shall dream dreams, your young men shall see visions:

"And also upon the servants and upon the handmaids in those days will I pour out my spirit.

"And I will shew wonders in the heavens and in the earth, blood, and fire, and pillars of smoke.

"The sun shall be turned into darkness, and the moon into the blood, before the great and the terrible day of the Lord come.

"And it shall come to pass, that whosoever shall call on the name of the Lord shall be delivered: for in mount Zion and in Jerusalem shall be deliverance, as the Lord hath said, and in the remnant whom the Lord shall call.

Joel then repeats his prophecy and again describes an army attacking Jerusalem, the battle of Armageddon. Joel then again describes scenes from the millennial reign of Christ; *"So shall ye know that I am the Lord your God dwelling in Zion, my holy mountain: then shall Jerusalem be holy, and there shall no strangers pass through her any more."*

Joel 3:1

"For, behold in those days, and in that time, when I shall bring again the captivity of Judah and Jerusalem,

I will also gather all nations, and will bring them down in to the valley of Jehoshaphat, and will plead with them there for my people and for my heritage Israel, whom they have scattered among the nations, and parted my land."

Joel 3:14

Multitudes, multitudes in the valley of decision: for the day of the Lord is near in the valley of decision.

The sun and the moon shall be darkened, and the stars shall withdraw their shining.

The Lord also shall roar out of Zion, and utter his voice from Jerusalem; and the heavens and the earth shall shake: but the Lord will be the hope of his people, and the strength of the children of Israel.

So shall ye know that I am the Lord your God dwelling in Zion, my holy mountain: then shall Jerusalem be holy, and there shall no strangers pass through her any more.

And it shall come to pass in that day, that the mountains shall drop down new wine, and the hills shall flow with milk, and all the rivers of Judah shall flow with waters, and a fountain shall come forth of the house of the Lord, and shall water the valley of shittim.

Egypt shall be a desolation, and Edom shall be a desolate wilderness, for the violence against the children of Judah, because they have shed innocent blood in their land.

But Judah shall dwell for ever, and Jerusalem from generation to generation.

For I will cleanse their blood that I have not cleansed: for the Lord dwelleth in Zion."

OTHER INTERESTING NOTES FROM AROUND THE WORLD

THE EVIL KINGDOM OF THE BEAST
(Some Additional Current Events For Consideration)

As mentioned before, one of the signs indicating the nearness of the Savior's return is that an evil kingdom of Satan would come forth, which corrupts and then dominates the world's kingdoms, initiates a world economy that it controls, persecutes and then kills the righteous and those who resist it. The question might be asked concerning the progress of this evil kingdom as it corrupts and dominates the world, including the United States.

As has always been the case with those that serve the cause of Satan and help build his kingdom, they always try to force their ways upon everyone else using whatever means possible to accomplish their goals, including deception (lies and deceits), bribery, murder, and even war. Their aim is to gain wealth, power and control over others. It has been that way since the time of Cain.

Undoubtedly, world communism and other secret or dark societies are just some of the major components of this great "kingdom of the beast" that the Bible has warned us in the last days will try (and succeed for the most part), in taking control of the world. Is there any further evidence that this socialistic/communistic New World Order has been successful in doing this in the world and perhaps in the United States? Again, the answer sadly is yes. As part of this New World Order plan, individual nations (and their citizens) must give up their individual freedoms and national sovereignty to those in control of this one world government. This has been the satanic goal since the beginning of time and is now represented by the socialist/communist/elitist. (Note: Contrary to popular opinion, the mainstream media and even our own government's declaration, communism is not dead. According to the highest ranking KGB officer ever to defect, Anatoliy Golitsyn (who defected in the late 1960s), he indicated that at that time world communism had embarked upon a daring 30+ year plan designed by the Soviet

KGB, that would entice their enemies NATO and the U.S. to disarm thus allowing them the opportunity to complete their world wide objective of conquering and controlling the world. (Which incidently is the same as Satan's desire.) This grand ruse would be to go through the motions to declare communism dead, embrace democracy, breakup the Soviet Union, disband part of the Soviet army, even dismantle the Berlin Wall, while at the same time infiltrate communist agents and sympathizers in high places in their enemies governments so that at the appropriate time they could quickly rearm and strike with very little resistance. This great ruse was announced and detailed by Golitsyn almost 10 years before the Berlin Wall came down. At the time, it was dismissed as totally unbelievable and yet since then everything that Golitsyn outlined has come to pass. A terrific book, but hard to obtain, is Golitsyn's "New Lies For Old" which describes this ruse.) One of the organizations that was created by the communists to assist in this goal is the United Nations. What follows is just a very small sample of the available indications of how far these goals have been accomplished here in the United States.

"Our task of creating a socialist America can only succeed when those who would resist us have been totally disarmed."[1]

"When personal freedom's being abused, you have to move to limit it. That's what we did in the announcement I made last weekend on the public housing projects, about how we're going to have weapon sweeps and more things like that to try to make people safer in their communities."[2]

"We can't be so fixated on our desire to preserve the rights of ordinary Americans."[3]

President Clinton, during a news conference on March 7, 1997, when specifically questioned about turning the sovereignty of the United States over to the United Nations, giving control over the army to the Russians, and turning over land to foreign nations, did not deny it as he was encouraged and expected to do, but

---

[1]*Sara Brady, The National Educator, January 1994 Issue, pg 3 (Note: A new gun control initiative is being introduced by Sara Brady/HCI and Representative McCarthy in June of 1998.)*

[2]*President Bill Clinton, on "Enough is Enough", MTV, March 22, 1994*

[3]*President Bill Clinton, USA Today, March 11, 1993, pg 2A*

instead said, "I would say there's a serious issue here that every American has to come to grips with.... the fact that we can no longer be an independent nation in the world today. In order to cooperate with the nations of the world,**"We're better off with NATO, we're better off with the United Nations."**[1]

Additionally, President Clinton has arranged for Communist China to take over the strategic military/industrial port of Long Beach to the point of actually spending over $70 million dollars to refit the port. Lately, there has been an unbelievable revelation that Clinton, overriding all of his security advisors, gave extremely sensitive missile technology to the Chinese to help improve their ICBM's, (of which a number are currently targeted at the United States.) This, while at the same time the Chinese have been arming the Iranians, a nation who is declared "at war" with the United States, with their version of a second generation Exocet anti-ship missile so that they could effectively destroy all US ships in the Persian Gulf in about 30 minutes[2]. The Chinese are also in the process of arming IRAQ with ballistic missiles capable of hitting Israel from farther away with greater accuracy, and have even been caught trying to sell thousands of AK-47s to the street gangs of Los Angeles.[3]

According to a recent Pentagon study[4], China believes that the U.S. is weak militarily and in decline as a superpower. "Worse still, Chinese military books and journals in the 1990s have begun to discuss the necessity of taking military action against a more powerful opponent in certain circumstances." **In describing US weakness, Chinese military writers asserted that the US barely won the Gulf War, that it could not contain Chinese power and had only a 30 per cent chance of winning a war in Asia. "We already see evidence that China considers a future war with the US sufficiently plausible to be openly discussed," the report said.** The report further stated that China believes that the US was actively trying to subvert and dismember China. More recent revelations tell us that the Chinese have targeted the United States with at least 13 ICBMs with nuclear warheads while at the same time bribing our nations highest officials to provide them with previous classified technology to improve their

---

[1]*From Bill Clinton's News Conference on Friday, 3-7-97, question and answer section.*

[2]*Information from Senator Bob Bennett, Senate subcommittee on Foreign Operations, April 1997. API*

[3]*In 1996 2000 AK-47s were discovered being smuggled to the LA gangs from a Chinese COSCO ship docked in San Francisco. COSCO is the CHinese Military's Maritime Navy.*

[4]*Dangerous Chinese Perceptions, Michael Pilsbury for the Pentagon's Office of Net Assessments. March 8,1998*

missile accuracy.

National & Worldwide Citizen Registration Programs

Again, in Revelations it indicates that this kingdom of the "Beast/Dragon" will gain control of the nations of the earth and persecute the righteous. As outlined previously, one of the signs of the nearness of the Savior's coming is this degenerate earthly kingdom controlled by Satan gaining control to the point of causing everyone to receive a mark in their forehead, or in their right hands, in order to buy or sell, and also causing all those who do not support it to be killed. Concerning a mark in the hand or forehead, it has been suggested that such a mark, required for identification/approval in order to buy or sell, could be a reference to a computer chip that is injected under the skin of animals and humans.

Such chips are now being used as a means to identify humans as well. The U.S. military is now starting to have military personnel implanted with chips the size of a rice grain in their hands instead of using dogtags. According to a recent article in Time Magazine *(The Future of Money* (April 27, 1998) such chips will be used to take the place of cash, credit cards, ATM cards, checks, insurance policies, drivers license, social security, medical history, etc. and how this chip will soon be implanted under the skin of citizens worldwide.

A step preceding such usage as a population control method would be the requirement of the collection of personal information and its storage on a universal/national identity card that everyone would be required to carry. Two recent US federal laws that have just been passed address both of these issues.

National ID card and citizen registration has now become new federal law

In September of 1996, President Clinton signed into law the "Illegal Immigration Reform and Immigrant Responsibility Act of 1996." On page 650 of the bill (Public Law 104-208, Part B, Title IV) is a federal mandate requiring all citizens, starting after October 1, 2000, to use a special type of drivers license for identification at all Federal Agencies. This then requires all of the states to change their driver's licenses to conform to the "standards developed by the Secretary of the Treasury," often referred to as "Biometic Identity Cards" which include digitized fingerprints, holograms, and/or computer chips, before October 1, 2000. Several states are reportedly in the process of beginning the implementation of this new national ID, card though in Alabama serious public opposition has sprung up.

Section 325 (D) of the new Federal 'Dead-Beat Dad" law (Welfare Reform Bill, Public Law 104-193 8/22/96) that was recently enacted, requires each state to set up a system to register and collect information on every employee/person working in the state; including all history of marriage/divorce, family, children, financial records, employment records, tax records, assets, licenses, debts, debtors, liabilities, social security, credit cards, property, etc. It would be a federal crime not to report this information for both the employee and their employer who did not register them. This information would then be shared with the Federal government so that it could be cross-referenced and checked against a national registry of all those who supposedly owe child support. If a person is found to owe child support, this agency would be automatically empowered to initiate immediate garnishing of a person's earnings, as well as their assets.

UNITED NATIONS TAKING OVER SOVEREIGNTY OF THE UNITED STATES

As mentioned before, former U.S. administrations, and especially the current administration, is in the process of granting more and more of the sovereignty of the United States to the United Nations. A few more examples of this type of activity follow:

U.N. CONTROL OVER U.S. MILITARY

As mentioned previously, there are approximately 330,000 active U.S. military under United Nations command or NATO command (which is becoming a sub-organization of the United Nations) in almost 40 different countries. Most of these activities are described as "peacekeeping" or "police" actions, not direct warfare. Many of our current soldiers are now wearing the United Nations insignia and operate under the UN flag, instead of the U.S. flag. Recently, a soldier tried to fight this issue, saying it was unconstitutional for a U.S. soldier to wear the UN patch instead of the U.S. patch. He was court-martialed for refusing to obey a direct order.

U.S. LAND BEING DESIGNATED AS U.N. BIO-RESERVE AREAS
A brief history:

In 1971, UNESCO (United Nations Educational, Scientific, Cultural Organization) announced a new plan and program called "The Wildlands Project" and the "Biosphere Reserve Program." (Section 10.4.2.2.3 of the United National Global Biodiversity Assessment). The objective of this plan was to put 23% of the

144

world, including 50% of the United States, into protected wilderness areas (called "bioregions") that would be forbidden to "human intrusion." Each of these "core wilderness areas" would be surrounded by a "buffer area" of limited and "strictly controlled human intrusion." Adjacent to these buffer zones would be designated areas for human "settlements" called "cooperation zones."

The foundation for this plan is summarized in the statement by Dr. Reed Noss, chief architect of the plan:

"The collective needs of non-human species must take precedence over the needs and desires of humans."[1]

UNESCO produced a World Heritage Treaty that it proposed all United Nations countries sign in order to implement this plan throughout the world.

The treaty design and plan was adopted by the United Nations general assembly (UN Resolution 2997) in December of 1972. As part of that resolution the United Nations created UNEP (United Nations Environmental Programme) to spearhead the worldwide implementation of the plan. Their outlined five step plan is summarized as follows:

1. Redraw land maps to differentiate biological characteristics rather than political jurisdiction.

2. Regroup human populations into self-sustaining settlements that minimize impact on biodiversity.

3. Educate humans in the "gaia ethic," which holds that Gaia is the creator of all life and all life is a part of the creator. ("The Mother Nature" or nature is the center of life concept.)

4. Create a new system of governance based on local decision-making within the framework of international agreements.

5. Reduce the use of natural resources by (a) reducing population; (b) reducing consumption; and (c) shifting to "appropriate" technology. (From

---

[1] "Rewilding America," eco-logic Magazine (Publ. By Environmental Conservation Organization, Hollow Rock, TN), November/December 1995, p.20.]

military/defense to programs that will "elevate humanity.")

The UNESCO World Heritage Treaty was signed by Richard Nixon in November 1972, even before its full adoption by the UN General Assembly. It was ratified by Congress and became effective in 1975, but had not been implemented much until Bill Clinton came into office.

In America, The President's Council on Sustainable Development (PCSD) was created by President Clinton's Executive Order # 12852 in 1993 and presented its report, *"Sustainable America, A New Consensus"* in 1995 under the direction of Vice President Al Gore.[1] It is a compilation of 154 action items patterned after the UN "Agenda 21" to be implemented in America. At the November, 1995 meeting of the PCSD, council members, who were also Clinton's cabinet members, announced that at least 67 of the action items could be implemented "administratively," without Congressional involvement. The document provides 16 "We Believe" statements which embrace the 27 principles articulated in the Rio Declaration from Earth Summit II. Among those statements are these:

"The election process and representative government created by the U.S. Constitution is clearly unacceptable to the PCSD."

"We need a new collaborative decision process that leads to better decisions; more rapid change; and more sensible use of human, natural, and financial resources in achieving our goals."

In 1995, UNEP proposed to the United States a "Convention on Biological Diversity" which Bill Clinton signed, but as of yet, has not been ratified by Congress. However, Bill Clinton and Al Gore have begun to implement the outlined plan the convention proposed (part of the UN World Heritage Treaty) for the United States under the PCSD and the U.S. MAN & BIOSPHERE (MAB) programs.

The objective of the program, conceived in 1971, has been to designate sites worldwide for preservation and to protect the biodiversity of chosen sites on a global level. Toward that end, North America has been divided into 21 "bioregions." In turn, each of the 21 bioregions has been divided into three zones:

---

[1]*See the Whitehouse PCSD web site at WWW..whitehouse.gov/ wh/eop/pcsd*

(1) Wilderness area, designated as habitat of plants and animals. Human habitation, use, or intrusion is forbidden.

(2) Buffer zones surrounding the wilderness areas. Limited, and strictly controlled, human access is permitted within this zone.

(3) Cooperation zones, the only zones where humans, in designated "settlements" will be permitted to live.

Because of the "resistance" of the United States citizens towards the sovereignty issue (ie. Giving up U.S. national sovereignty to the United Nations), as mentioned in the "Report of the Commission on Global Governance," to whit:

> **"The impulse to possess turf is a powerful one for all species; yet it is one that people must overcome. Sensitivity over the relationship between international responsibility and national sovereignty [is a] considerable obstacle to the leadership at the international level. Sovereignty is a principle which will yield only slowly and reluctantly to the imperatives of global environmental cooperation."[1]**

[Note: The plan is to convene a World Conference on Global Governance in 1998, similar to the Earth Summit that was held in Rio de Janeiro in 1992. Official world governance treaties are expected to come out of that conference, with the goal of worldwide implementation by the year 2000. For the most part they have been already published in an official document offered to the world, entitled, "Our Global Neighborhood: The Report of the Commission on Global Governance." http://www.cgg.ch/CHAP1.html>. Oxford University Press, ISBN0-19-827997-3, 410 pages.], the convention outlined a proposed implementation plan for the U.S.[2]

1) Start with a seemingly innocent-sounding program like the "World Heritage Areas in Danger." Bring all human activity under regulation in a 14-18 million acre buffer zone around Yellowstone National Park.

---

[1] *"Report of the Commission on Global Governance," eco-logic Magazine (publ. By Environmental Conservation Organization, Hollow Rock, TN), January/February 1996, p.4.*

[2]*Based on United Nations World Heritage Program; United Nations Convention on Biological Diversity, Article 8a-e; United Nations Global Biodiversity Assessment, Section 10.4.2.2.3; U.S. Man and the Biosphere Strategic Plan (1994 draft); U.S. Heritage Corridors Program; and "The Wildlands Project," (published in Wild Earth, Dec. 1992). Also, see Science, "The High Cost of Biodiversity," Vol. 280, June 25, 1993, pp.1868-1871.*

2) Next, declare all federal land (except Indian reservations) as buffers, along with private land within federal administration boundaries.

3) Next, extend the U.S. Heritage corridor buffer zone concept along major river systems. Begin to convert critical federal lands and ecosystems to these zones/bioreserves.

4) Finally, convert all U.S. Forest Service, grasslands, and wildlife refuges to reserves. Add additional reserves and corridors so that 50 percent of landscape is preserved.

Part of the implementation of the above plan was the designation of the 47 national parks and monuments, as United Nations Bioreserve Areas. One of the main Bioreserve areas is Yellowstone National Park. The Park has been designated as a UN Biosphere reserve that excludes humans. The federal government, in accordance to the UN outline, is in the process of creating a "buffer zone" that surrounds the Park. This is being called the **Columbian Basin Ecosystem Management Plan**, and is in its final stages with comments due by October 6th 1997 on the preferred alternative to "actively restore" 144 million acres. The federal ecosystem covers all of Idaho, half of Washington and Oregon and parts of Montana. The plan was initiated by a Clinton administration's memorandum of understanding with 21 federal agencies after the Biodiversity Treaty failed in the Senate over two years ago. The memorandum allows the agencies to bypass congressional authority and oversight. Under the new plan, the federal agencies are expected to rewrite existing land use plans, cut grazing and timber permits, identify road closures and many other aggressive actions. Although they claim property rights will not be affected, the preferred alternative is based on the premise that "the best resource areas are those with no development of any kind," and it is their goal to restore the Columbia basin to this pristine level. The releasing of wolves back into the area is also part of the process. Another example was the designation of the Utah Grand Staircase-Escalante area as protected federal land by presidential decree.

The legal status of biodiversity has been further elevated by Vice President Gore's "Ecosystem Management Policy," which places biodiversity protection at the same priority level as human health, and which further instructs officials to consider human beings to be a "biological resource" in all ecosystem management activities.

148

American Heritage Rivers Act

Another larger step is that President Bill Clinton and Vice President Al Gore have enacted, again as a Presidential Executive Order, the AMERICAN HERITAGE RIVERS INITIATIVE, which needed no congressional ratification to become law. This new law will allow the Federal Government, and other non-U.S. organizations, to nominate and designate 10 rivers annually to be protected under this new program. The first five rivers for 1998 that President Clinton has proposed are the Upper Missisippi River from Minnesota to St. Louis, the Connecticut River in New England, the Yellowstone River in Wyoming, the French Borad River in North Carolina and Tennessee, and the Willanette River in Oregon. The Presidential directive proposes to select and control rivers for "natural, historic, cultural, social, economic and ecological diversity."

When a river is so designated, inclusion will be permanent and can include the entire watershed, including all tributaries, wetlands, public and private property. (Very similar to current wetlands regulations, the California Coastal Authority, and the Endangered Species Act.)

The management of the river will be under the direct control of a federally appointed director (called a "Navigator") whose authority will supercede all local, regional, and state authority in overseeing any and all use of the water and land that is included in the designated area. Aerial photography, satellite surveillance, and federal marshalls will be used to police and expand the program.

EPA

Another story similar to the one above could be written concerning the United States Environmental Protection Agency. Again, just recently, new federal regulations have been issued, increasing the standards that must be met by citizens and communities. The penalties for committing an environmental crime are often more severe than if a person committed rape or murder.

ECONOMIC BONDAGE & DEPRESSION

Of course one of the ways that a government can gain control over their people is to subjugate them by economic means. In order to do this, the government (or the organization that wishes to do the controlling) needs to gain control of the currency of the people it wishes to subjugate. It then can manipulate the currency and the economy to achieve its desired result. In the United States, for example, this has already been accomplished when in 1913 a private company, owned by the international bankers, called the Federal Reserve Bank, was given this control over the U.S. currency. (The Federal Reserve Bank is primarily owned by non U.S. citizens.) The results of this can be seen today in the family life of every American. Sixty years ago it took the average family only one person working, usually the father, to provide for the family. This left the mother home to nurture and care for the children. It now takes an average of 2 persons per household to provide for the family (even though the family is smaller in number). Experts are indicating that within the next 10 years it will take 3 average wage earners to provide for the needs of a family.

Note: According to the Bureau of Labor Statistics, the average full time worker is making less and less money as the United States moves into a post-industrial economy. For example, Wal-Mart just replaced General Motors as the largest private business employer in America.. The average motor vehicle employee earned $847.19 per week, while the average retail worker earned $237.69 per week. The IRS reports that in 1994, 50% of the households in the U.S. reported a combined income of less that $22,000 gross annual income.

This economic bondage has contributed greatly to the disintegration of the family, which has also been aided by the immoral attitudes and laws that have been fostered by the U.S. leadership (many who are active, others who are unwitting agents of the Kingdom of the Beast).

So great has this family disintegration become, not only in the United States, but worldwide (mainly because the influence of the kingdom of the Beast has grown so strong), that youth crime has become the single largest crime growth area. Divorce, abuse, immorality, increased violence, drugs, etc. can all be directly associated with the breakup of the family.

Immorality, especially homosexuality & lesbianism, sexual perversions of every unimaginable kind, and general wickedness and evil continually were prophesied to be rampant in the last days just prior to Jesus's return. Almost all of these things are being encouraged, showcased or forced by those in power throughout the world, while the opposing force of the family is being systematically destroyed. (See "Promoting Immorality By The State" in the Appendix) (Remember their watch-cry is, "it takes a village" to raise children, when it should be, "it takes a family.") All of these evil "fruits" indicate which spiritual kingdom is in control. Truly, evil is called good and good is called evil so that those trying to serve Jesus and keep His commandments are persecuted greatly. How long before this kingdom of the beast progresses from persecution to outright murder of the righteous, is not far distant. (Some would even say that it has already begun.)

PROMOTING IMMORALITY BY THE "STATE"

There are so many examples, but here is a recent one that so clearly demonstrates what is going on:

Washington State University Invites Children to Homosexual Conference

Directors of the Washington Conservative Caucus reacted sharply today upon learning that Washington State University is inviting junior high students from around the state to participate in a three-day conference on homosexuality described by the university as "kind of a Camp Queer experience."

"This is so bizarre it is beyond belief", said Rep. Bob Sump (R-Republic)."It is completely reprehensible for WSU to be inviting children to the university for a public celebration of immorality."

"Utterly amazing," agreed WCC chairman, John Koster (R-Monroe), "If I hadn't seen the email announcement myself, I couldn't believe that Washington State University could sink this low. Evidently the university has simply not contemplated the consequences of squandering its moral authority. I can only hope that parents around this state are alert to what their children are finding on the internet, and take a close look at the invitation before packing their children off to Pullman."

The WSU homosexual conference is planned for June 19-21, 1998 and targets "Gay, Lesbian, Bisexual, Transsexual", and "Questioning" high school and junior high students. WSU has confirmed this "Camp Queer experience" is a WSU program rather than a student body program. The university has advertised the camp by email, is sending flyers to schools and youth agencies, and has stated "we ... hope to attract as many junior high- and high-school aged youth from the Pacific Northwest as we can."

None of this surprises Senator Val Stevens (R-Arlington). "We have always known that recruitment of children into the lifestyle was central to the homosexual agenda," said Stevens. "But they have always denied it. Here is the smoking pistol of the Big Lie."

In a letter of May 27 to university President Sam Smith, Rep. Marc Boldt (R-Vancouver) expressed concerns regarding liability issues including parental consent, homosexual recruitment, and contraction of STDs, including AIDS. Rep. Sump echoed Rep. Boldt's concerns. "Marc is right on target with his concerns regarding the liability questions. First OK Boys Ranch, then Wenatchee, and now this -- a state university coaxing children into homosexual conduct.

Y2K...The Millennium Bug

WHAT IS THE Y2K COMPUTER PROBLEM OR BUG?

Simply: Testing has shown that almost all computer programs written before 1996 (approximately 97% of the computer software in the world), will simply either shut down or go haywire on January 1, 2000 unless a programming problem (with the 2000 date) is fixed. The promised 'quick fixes' haven't worked. With billions of lines of 'computer code' to fix, there are simply not enough computer programmers in the world to get the job done in time.

Example 1:
> In late 1997 IBM just told the FAA that all of the 20+ year old IBM 3038 mainframe computers that run all of the radar and air traffic control centers in the U.S. will shut down on 1/1/2000. They cannot be fixed in time (very few know the old machine Cobol language anymore), and therefore must be replaced. If a massive effort was undertaken immediately they could possibly be replaced in five years. On October 11, 1997, KLM (Northwest) Airlines subsequently announced that on 1/1/2000 most of its airplanes will be grounded until the problem is fixed. American Airlines and others have indicated that they will also have no choice but to do the same.

Example 2:
> *"Banks and other financial institutions generally will go bonkers if they don't fix their problem... In the worst case scenario, the entire financial infrastructure, including the stock market, will go haywire. Balances, records, and transactions will be lost...* **Y2K could be the event that could all but paralyze the planet."** ("*The Day the World Shuts Down,"*Newsweek,

June 2, 1997)   Some banks will be ready, but most won't, including the U.S. treasury. Even with the most optimistic outlook, there is a certainty that most people will have problems accessing their funds and investments. The great *"CASHLESS SOCIETY"* and Global Economy will come to a screeching halt for several months or years. Asian and European banking systems are even lagging behind the American system. Goldman Sachs recently said "It is already clear that the combined expertise of Europe's computing services industries will not be sufficient to address the problem:"

Example 3:

The Federal OMB's (Office of Management and Budget) 1997 fourth quarter report shows the following:

AGENCY	ESTIMATED COMPLIANCE DATE
Dept of Labor & Energy	2019
Dept of Defense	2012
Dept of Transportation	2010 (Including FAA)
Dept of Treasury	2004
Dept of Justice	2001
FEMA	2000.5

(Note: other independent sources such as the GAO and Senator Horne put these dates as extremely optimistic, not realistic.)

Example 4:

The U.S Railroad system, now entirely computerized, will shut down on 1/1/2000.   Even with the most optimistic scenario, there will be complete gridlock for months starting in the middle of winter. Most cities in the U.S. are dependent upon the railroads for coal, petroleum, heating oil, chemicals and food... including the coal and fuel oil that runs most of the electric power plants in the U.S.

Example 5:

The U.S. Power Grid is also completely computerized and won't be ready since less than 5% have even started seriously working on the project. (A perfect example of 'Too Little...Too Late') The best case is massive regional power outages that could last from several days/weeks...up to months. The current outlook is that power outages could even start several months earlier.

Example 6:

The SEC (Security and Exchange Commission) has just started requesting reports from public companies on their Y2K progress in an effort to keep stock holders informed. The first reports indicate that things are looking extremely bad. In the report of the first quarter of 1998, of the 250 largest companies in the U.S., 15% have not even started working on the problem and 58% have not even finished the assessment phase (usually a 1-2 year process of testing the systems to see which ones will be effected by the Y2K bug). Almost all corporations who have begun working on the Y2K problem, find out that the problem will affect their operations much more severely than at first anticipated or imagined.

IMPORTANT BIBLE NOTE: **While the Y2K problem/event is not specifically mentioned in the Bible (as far as I can determine), the experience will be a perfect trial for preparing for other future events which are described. There is also the VERY DISTINCT POSSIBILITY that the Y2K event could possibly lead to other events that are specifically mentioned in the Bible, such as perhaps the 13 month world war. (Remember, the U.S./NATO/South Korea military is a technology based military, while the military of the Chinese, Russians, Iranians, Iraqis, and North Koreans is not. In essence, the United States and most of her allies will be next to completely defenseless because of the Y2K problems.)**

If China, Russia, Iraq, Iran, North Korea, etc. decided to attack/invade another country, including the United States, there would be very little we could do to stop them except arm the citizens and fight them hand to hand. (Which is what George Washington said he saw in his vision.) In the parable of the ten virgins, the virgins were waiting with some only partially prepared (the foolish) with the expectation that when things started to happen they would then finish their preparations. However, when things finally did get moving, it happened so suddenly and so quickly that they did not have time to prepare, but were left out. **You can always be prepared too early (which can be of great comfort), but there is no such thing as being prepared too late.** It is my opinion that the Y2K problem could be the trigger or start which leads to many of the final events of the last days as described in the Bible.

WHAT CAN YOU DO TO PREPARE?

The most important thing is to begin to act quickly but wisely. It will not be long before the general public, especially next year, will begin to understand the true consequences/impact of the year 2000 problem. Expect prices, etc. to go up at that time. Some ideas to consider:

1. Prepare your family first
   ●GET OUT OF DEBT AS MUCH AS POSSIBLE. (And stay out!)
   ●With the potential banking/financial market collapse starting perhaps as early as mid 1999 (or perhaps sooner), discuss the safety of your investments with your financial advisor.
   ●Prepare your family physically to survive for several months. (But don't go into debt.) Consider the following issues in light of it possibly being a severe winter:
   *Heat (heat for warmth and also for cooking)
   *Water (for at least a few weeks.)
   *Food
   *Security/safety (If you live in a big city...perhaps you might want to visit the relatives who live out on the farm during the holidays, etc.)
   *Sanitation
   *Medical (perhaps look into natural methods, herbs, etc since modern medicine is based on technology. Also have enough critical medicines in storage)
   ●Obtain seeds (non-hybrid) to grow a garden. Prepare a garden place now.

2. Warn your friends, neighbors and family. (Some will believe you, others will get the message in a few months.) Try to surround yourself with good neighbors and friends. During hard times, good trustworthy friends will be worth their weight in gold, and could make the difference between survival or not.

3. Consider the possibility of how the Y2K problem might affect your work/employment. Some businesses will hardly be affected, some will be greatly enhanced, while others will be severely affected negatively. Prepare accordingly.

SURVIVAL TIPS/HINTS

Y2K SPECIAL EVENT DATES

One of the most concise timetable listings of probable events concerning the Y2K computer problems is contained in an excerpt that I found on the internet. It is most enlightening. Contributed by: Julius Marinaro E-mail:Julius.Marinaro@state.co.us   16 March 1998   (Other places to obtain information concerning Y2K would be WWW.GaryNorth.com. and WWW.year2000.com)

TIME LINE FOR DISASTER 2000

1. INTRODUCTION The biggest problem I have had in planning for the Year 2000 Millennium Bug Disaster is the lack of a Big Picture of exactly what will happen and when it will happen. In fact, nobody knows this, because there are many variables and unknowns.

For example, when the Big Day (January 1, 2000) arrives, we expect a lot of computer systems to fail, but the picture is not that simple. The actual failure date will depend on the specific type of technology and its operation schedule. Computer programs which run on mainframes come in different date flavors. There are Year-end programs and Month-end programs and Quarterly programs and Daily programs. So each such program might not fail until it is actually operated. In other words, the Bomb will not go off entirely at one single time. There have already been many sporadic system failures due to the Y2K problem, and I expect there will be sporadic and unpredictable failures in 1999 and 2000. Even if a massive amount of systems fail on the Big Day, that will not be the only day on which Y2K failures occur.

But who is going to risk operating computer based technology during this time period if they know the dangers? By the time the Big Day rolls around, the people in charge will know that they face massive liability lawsuits if they operate flawed systems. It would be   cheaper for them to declare bankruptcy, or suspend operations for awhile. So for mainframe programs (which large corporations and large   government agencies use heavily), we might reasonably expect only remediated programs to be run, or possibly reversion to fall back systems, or possibly suspension of computer operations until repairs are completed. In other words, only the most critical programs might be operating, if at all, seriously limiting the business of large corporations and agencies.

Even with these unknowns, it seemed a good idea to piece together my version of the Big Picture, in order to make my plans. What follows is my best guess at what might happen, it is just one alternative future, and the future is not cast in concrete.

2. SIGNIFICANT DATES

Following is a list of known Thresholds of Failure and other significant dates for the next few years. (A Threshold of Failure is a known date of Y2K failure for a specific technology, unless it is remediated.) These dates were obtained from Internet documents and other Y2K sources.

January 1, 1999 - There are many computer based systems which project forward one calendar year in order to do their work for the current calendar year. In addition, the Electric Power Research Institute has stated that it has identified some electric industry systems which will fail on this date, unless remediated.

Anytime, 1999 - Potential for computer system failures. Some older mainframe computer programs use the two-digit year '99 to mark the end-of-file (end of the input data stream for processing). When this year appears in legitimate transactions for processing, these programs might stop processing at the start of the data stream and be unable to process transactions, unless remediated.

April 1, 1999 - This is not an April Fool's joke. The fiscal year for Canada and New York State both start on April 1. If their fiscal management software is not remediated by this date, their ability to function might be diminished. It might happen at a later date, depending on when the software is operated. Considering both Canada and New York have large welfare systems, this problem could give us a preview of what will happen to other welfare systems when their new fiscal year starts.

July 1, 1999 - The fiscal year for many other American states start on July 1, including Colorado. If their fiscal management software is not remediated by this date, their ability to function might be diminished. How would welfare recipients react if aid were cut off?

August 22, 1999 - The Global Positioning System (GPS) resets itself. Any GPS device may give incorrect date and position unless repaired or replaced. Some banks use GPS receivers to mark the time on big (Billion Dollars) loans in order to compute interest correctly.

September 9, 1999 - Potential for computer system failures. Some older mainframe computer programs use the specific date of 9/9/99 to mark the end-of-file (end of the input data stream for processing). When this date appears in legitimate transactions for processing, these program might stop processing part way in the data stream and be unable to process remaining transactions.

In addition, this same date is used in some older computer programs as a special code to end retention of archived data (historical data, such as your financial records, which were to be kept forever). If these programs are run on or after this date, the archived data will be deleted, so some computerized records about you may disappear prematurely.

October 1, 1999 - The U.S. federal fiscal year starts on October 1. If the federal fiscal management software is not remediated by this date, their ability to operate might stop. What would happen to our welfare system and how would welfare recipients react?

Second Half, 1999 - Potential for societal disruptions and breakdowns due to panic. I presume the mass of Americans have their heads stuffed in the sand on the Y2K problem. What I predict will happen is based on the notion of spaced repetition. If you hear a statement only once, you might not believe it. But if you hear it repeated six or seven times spaced out over a long time span, it will finally sink in. What I suggest will happen is that if we have a series of well publicized system crashes every month or so starting this year, the general public will finally wake up and then panic. At such a time, I would expect runs on food stores and banks, possibly leading to shortages of basic commodities (including paper money) which would lead to rationing. In my humble opinion, the most likely time for public panic would be the October/November time frame. I expect a national state of emergency to be declared, and possibly martial law in urban areas.

December 31, 1999 - The FAA was informed by IBM that 40 of its computers used to display air traffic control data on computer screens will cease functioning on January 1, 2000. Reports have appeared that perhaps twenty-five to fifty per cent of flights will be grounded.

The U.S. Army is scheduled to finish remediation of its logistic computers on this date. If they fail, the results are world shaking. You see, military logistics are the muscles behind a war machine. If there is no food, no guns and no ammunition for the military, there is no army. If there is no U.S. Army, there is no U.S. foreign policy and no troops to enforce martial law at home.

January 1, 2000 - The Big Day. Embedded computer systems (microchips implanted in devices), would fail on a schedule determined by the specific application. Certainly some will fail today, but others may not fail for days, weeks or months based on their maintenance schedule and other factors. Emergency damage control should start on or about this date, if not sooner due to societal disruptions. This seems a likely date for electric power utilities to fail if they haven't already reduced operations or unplugged non-critical customers.

In my humble opinion, the entire month of January will have Y2K related failures, not just the first few days or the first week, and possibly martial law in urban areas.

February 1, 2000 - According to Mr. Capers Jones of Software Productivity Research, lawyers will start damage assessment and litigation filing for the massive amount of damages which occur due to Y2K. He states this will continue through July of 2000.

In my view, February will start a period of alternating after shocks and calms through the first half of 2000. Each episode of after shock or calm could last up to a month.

February 29, 2000 - Leap Year. In addition to the Y2K failure, many computers may not be able to handle the leap year, if they are used on this date.

Spring, 2000 - Growing season starts. If lots of farmers are bankrupt by this time, and their seed suppliers are out of business, and the transportation network is diminished, and the food distribution system is inoperative, we face a serious food shortage for 2000 into 2001.

May 5, 2000 - Planetary Alignment Day. According to astronomers, the Earth will line up opposite the Sun from the other planets on this day, more or less in a line. The concern is that the total gravitational forces of the other planets may cause crustal changes (earthquakes) in the Earth. Not a good thing if our disaster relief agencies are overloaded from Y2K.

August 1, 2000 - According to Mr. Capers Jones of Software Productivity Research, businesses will start recovery from Y2K damage and replacement of defective computers, programs, systems, etc. He states this will continue through December of 2000. I interpret his statement to be an implication that large portions of American business will be out of commission for most of the year 2000.

My calculations for the timing of each phase are: a) The Y2K Disaster phase should start in earnest about October/November 1999 due to public panic. The crescendo should be the whole month of January 2000, followed by a period of after shocks and calms lasting through July, 2000. That's eight to ten months of critical conditions. b) Assuming the two-to-one ratio mentioned above, the Y2K Recovery phase should last about sixteen to twenty months, ending sometime between November 2001 and March 2002. Economic Downturn - During the recovery phase in the above examples, there were depressions and other economic malaise. Jobs may be scarce along with basic commodities and utilities. Prepare for this prospect.

WHERE TO GET FOOD STORAGE

Almost all of the experts who have studied what goes on when things go awry such as disasters, economic recessions/depressions, major societal changes, etc indicate one of the best ways to prepare and then survive such changes or disasters, is to have a years supply of food and other items on hand. So many place have run out of food storage of late, that it is almost a week to week basis. One of the best books on the subject, complete with a list of food storage places for every state is "Making the Best of Basics, Family Preparedness Handbook" by James Talmage Stevens, published by Gold Leaf Press, tenth edition. Beyond that, rather than print lists of something that would soon be in error, I will provide a free 800 number....1-877-527-8329... and a web site that will have current food storage information on it.

WHITE BUFFALO, SIOUX PROPHECY HERALDING THE MILLENIUM, IS BORN

Many of the plains Indians, including the Sioux, Oneida, Cherokee, Navaho, Ojibwa, Winnebago, Lakota and Lac du Flambou tribes have a similar tradition and prophecy concerning a white buffalo calf which, when born, would indicate that the time for great change, renewal and goodness was very near. No white buffalo birth has been recorded for over 50 years, and the National Buffalo Association had believed the gene needed to produce a white calf had been lost when the buffalo had been nearly driven to extinction. They estimated that the odds were on the order of 1 in 10 million. However, the world was stunned when a "miracle" occurred in September of 1994 as a pure white calf was born to otherwise "normal (dark)" parents. Spiritual leaders from over 30 Indian tribes have visited and declared the white calf the sacred prophesy coming true.

The Sioux tradition is summarized as follows: Seven generations ago during a time of much famine and dissent among the Indian nations, a beautiful Indian maiden, clad in white buckskin, appeared and told the chiefs and elders that she had been sent by the creator to offer goodness and peace to the people. She brought the buffalo for food and presented them the first sacred peace pipe telling them how to use it to pray and bring peace to the Indian Nations. She told the women and children that what they were doing was as great as the warriors. As she left she rolled on the ground and became a white buffalo calf . At that time, the prophets predicted that the white buffalo calf would return in seven generations, in a time of chaos and disparity, to help heal the dissent of the people, unifying all of the races (black, white, red and yellow), bringing out goodness and peace, returning spirituality to all men, and healing Mother Earth from great pollutions. As a sign to know the right calf, it would start out white, turn to yellow, then black, then red, (to represent all of the people), and then to white again when the races became purified.

It is reported that many of the tribal elders had received visions during the few years prior to the calf's birth, predicting its birth and waiting for it with great anticipation. Since its birth in 1994, it has changed colors from white to yellow, to black and then to red in 1996.[1]

"THE BIBLE CODE"

The book called "The Bible Code" brings up a very interesting question, "could God perhaps inspire ancient prophets, specifically Moses, to leave a hidden code in the Bible as perhaps a further prophetic warning for our time?"   Since "The Bible Code" book has been discussed a great deal in the public lately, especially in relation to the Last Days, I include a brief synopsis of it so that the reader can gain an understanding and pursue the above question for themselves.

Over 50 years ago, a Rabbi in Czechoslovakia, played around with the idea of taking the Torah (the five books of Moses in Hebrew) and checking to see if there was anything to find by counting every 3rd, 5th , 10th, etc. letter and adding them together. He painstakingly put all of the Hebrew letters of the 1st book, Genesis, on sheets of paper and then noticed that if he skipped every 50 letters, he found the Hebrew word "TORAH" spelled out at the beginning of Genesis. He also found out that it was also spelled out in the beginning of Exodus, Numbers, and Deuteronomy. As a novice mathematician, he knew that this was very significant, and something that happened not by chance, it had to have been intentionally put there, "by God." He wrote a little about his discovery and it was forgotten.

About 12 years ago, a world famous Israeli mathematician, Dr. Eliyahu Rips, heard about it and decided to investigate. He put the Hebrew letters of "Genesis" into the computer and asked it to start checking for word sequences. There were thousands of them. He then picked some words and had the computer print them out so that they lined up (top to bottom) and then looked at the letters surrounding the key word. He then found associated phrases, dates, words, etc. that all pertained to the key word, including modern day names, and events. Statistically, he deduced, it was impossible for these things to be randomly created and associated. Therefore, it had to have been placed there, on purpose, by some incredibly intelligent, superior being as messages/warnings to us in the "end of days." He felt, being a very religious man, that God, through Moses, had perhaps left us some very important messages in code, and that only now, with the help of

---

[1] *See several articles starting in 1994 in the Beloit Daily News (Wisconsin), Neal White Editor. Do WWW search on "white buffalo"*

computers, would we be able to decipher and understand them. He presented a scientific paper to a major science/mathematics journal on the code where it was confirmed by a battery of skeptical mathematicians to be correct.

A U.S. reporter heard about this and investigated. He became so convinced of the reality of this "bible code" that in September 1994 he sent a letter to Yitshak Rabin, Prime Minister of Israel, telling him that the code indicated he would be assassinated during the Jewish year starting in September 1995 by a person named "Amir," "one of his people" in Tel Aviv. He even flew to Israel to warn Rabin personally, believing that the outcome could be changed, but was not granted audience with Rabin. Of course his letter and he were ignored until on November 4, 1995 Yitshak Rabin was shot from behind by Yigal Amir, an Israeli, in Tel Aviv exactly as the bible code had described. The "bible code" also predicted that "Netanyahu" would become the next Prime Minister in 1996, and contrary to all pollsters and experts, Benjamin Netanyahu was surprisingly elected on May 19, 1996 over Shimon Peres in the closest Israeli election in the country's history (50.4% vs 49.6%).

The book, "The Bible Code" by Michael Drosnin, is extremely fascinating and makes for interesting reading. For example, using the quotes found in the "bible code" indicates that the "next war," "it will be after the death of the Prime Minister," "all his people to war," "world war," "third," "atomic holocaust" that begins initially in "Jerusalem" by a terrorist attack from "Libya" in the Jewish year of 5760 (the year 2000) with the date "9th of Av is the day of the third" or July 25, specifically mentioned. This date is significant for the Jews in that it was the day that Jerusalem was destroyed by the Babylonians in 586 B.C. and again the second time by the Romans in 70 A.D.. It is a day known for tragedy and disaster for the Jews, and is often a day of fasting for the religious. (The other dates that coincide with "atomic holocaust" is the Hebrew year equivalent to 1945, [the year Hiroshima and Nagasaki were bombed] and the year 2006.) It also mentions four countries, Syria, Russia, China and U.S.A., and that the "allies" of Syria would be "Persia" and "Phut," the modern day countries of Iran and Libya. It also indicates that Netanyahu will be killed/murdered in war/battle before he reaches age 50. (Netanyahu will be 50 in the year 2000.)

Two other interesting points,
   1. The "bible code" indicates that associated with the phrase "great earthquake" are the countries of the United States, Japan, China & Israel with future dates, 2000, 2006 and 2113. Phrases that cross with Japan, the country most closely associated with "great earthquake" are "economic collapse,"

"earthquake struck Japan," the years 2000 and 2006, and "year of the plague." The "bible code" also indicated that "Kobe" was associated with the words "earthquake," "fire," "the big one" and the year 1995. (Kobe was struck by a major earthquake and fire in 1995.) As was "S.F. Calif." associated with "fire, earthquake," "city consumed, destroyed" and the year 1906. (San Francisco was destroyed by an earthquake and fire in 1906.) As was also "China," "great earthquake," and the year 1976. (In 1976 China was struck with the deadliest earthquake in world history when an estimated 800,000 Chinese died.)

2. The "bible code" indicates that associated with the word "comet" are the phrases "starlike object," "Its path struck their dwelling," "year predicted for the world" and the year 2006. Also the year 2010 and comet appear with the phrases "days of horror" "darkness" and "gloom." The phrases, "Earth annihilated" and "It will be crumbled, driven out, I will tear it to pieces" appears with the date 2012.

The question remains, could God perhaps inspire ancient prophets, specifically Moses, to leave a hidden code in the Bible as perhaps a further prophetic warning for our time?

A Personal Note and Comment:
As I look and consider the signs and events that are happening around us, read the scriptures and ponder them together, the next few years leading up to and including the year 2000 stand out especially. **There seems to me to be a trend that many of these signs point to the year 2000 as being extremely significant and <u>cataclysmic</u>.** A few examples: the Russians are building new nuclear bomb shelters that will be finished by the year 2000; most of the computer systems of the United States (including defense systems) will be inoperative because of the year 2000 computer problems; many of the Jews are making plans to destroy the Dome of the Rock Mosque and begin building the Third Temple in the year 2000 (because the red heifer will be eligible for sacrifice); United Nations plans for world disarmament, Bio-regions, etc. are to be finished by the year 2000; there will be extremely significant signs in the heavens in the year 2000; the "Bible Code" hints of world war and atomic holocaust starting in Jerusalem in the year 2000, and on and on.

I also personally believe that the next few years will see some significant, traumatic changes, especially here in the United States, and if we haven't prepared ourselves, both spiritually and physically before they happen, it will be increasingly difficult, if not nearly impossible, to do so.

One simple possible example: A collapse in the U.S. Stock Market (whether initiated by a natural disaster of some kind, an "engineered" correction, the Asian financial collapse, or perhaps even as a result of the year 2000 computer glitch), which would trigger not only a dramatic U.S. economic collapse, but a worldwide economic collapse as well, is a very real possibility. It is interesting to note that currently the majority of the monies being put into the stock market are from middle-income America, not the super wealthy. (In fact, indications arc that the super wealthy are the ones who are in the process of selling to these newcomers, and for the most part, getting out of the stock market... not a good sign.)

Unless people had prepared themselves by following the counsel of the many advisors who have analyzed the situation (such as Don McAlvany, Gary North and many others), by getting out of all unnecessary debt and having a year's supply of food, etc., it would be extremely difficult to not fall into the trap of depending upon the government for assistance. If the economy did not recover quickly (a very strong probability), the longer the dependence upon the government lasted, the greater the dependence or bondage would become, perhaps leading to the financial mark of the beast being implemented.

There are several other scenarios that could lead to the same result, specifically a strong recession/depression that forces many to become in bondage to the government, and so in my opinion, the bottom line is thus (again), we should not delay, but begin our preparations in earnest, immediately, but with order and wisdom.

INDEX

666 . . . . 44, 53, 54

Adultery 110, 120, 122

Africa 69, 80

AIDS 29, 60, 152

Albania 73

Angel 60-65, 67-70, 83, 88, 92, 93, 109, 116, 117, 130

Apostle 21, 65

Apostle(s) . . . 3, 65, 127, 140, 143, 144, 165

Armageddon . 36, 41, 44, 45, 55, 58, 68, 71, 73, 76, 77, 79, 81, 89-92, 97, 114, 120, 136, 139

Atomic 62, 164

Beast . . 15-18, 21-23, 41-44, 46, 52, 54-56, 59, 60, 64, 68, 78, 79, 81, 91, 92, 117, 140, 150, 151, 165

Berlin Wall 141

Bible Code 163

Bio-reserve 144

Brady 141

Buffer Zones 145, 147

California 149

Charity 104, 108

Chernobyl 62, 63

Cherokee 161

China 142, 154, 163, 164

Chip 53, 143

Christ . . . . 0, v, vi, 1, 3, 7-11, 16, 19, 20, 25, 26, 36-39, 41, 45, 48, 50-52, 60, 76-79, 82, 89, 93, 100, 101, 104, 105, 107-109, 113, 115, 117, 120, 124, 126, 127, 131, 132, 139

Clinton 52, 141-143, 146, 148, 149

Comet 33, 34, 87, 99, 100, 164

Communism . . . 46, 48-50, 80, 140, 141

Computer . . . 53, 63, 143, 152, 156-159, 162, 164, 165

Cooperation Zones 147

Czechoslovakia 20, 46, 162

Daniel . 8, 13, 15-17, 19, 20, 26, 36, 38, 41, 55, 56, 76, 116, 129-132, 135, 136

Dead 61, 68, 81, 82, 88, 89, 93, 97, 101-104, 118, 140, 141

Devil 8, 36, 39, 71, 117

Disarmament 164

Dome of the Rock 94, 96, 164

Dragon 42-44, 68, 78

Earthquake 24, 26, 30, 58, 61, 81-84, 86-90, 93, 97-99, 120, 164

Eclipses 33

Economic . . . 40, 47, 48, 50, 52, 80, 121, 149, 150, 160, 165

Egypt 22, 23, 25, 59, 73, 81, 87, 92, 129, 133-135, 139

Elders 136, 137

Endangered Species 149

Environmental 145, 147, 149

EPA 149

Europe . . . 15, 16, 19, 20, 25, 28, 38, 41, 42, 45, 46, 48, 49, 51, 52, 55-57, 62, 69, 73, 74, 83

Evil . . . 4, 5, 16, 20, 22, 25, 35-37, 39-41, 50, 54, 55, 60, 65, 72, 79, 82-84, 114, 115, 120, 122-126, 137, 140, 150

Faith 52, 108, 109, 111, 118

False Prophet . . 44, 45, 51, 68, 71, 77-79, 81, 92

Family . . . ii, 50, 80, 120, 144, 150, 155

Food Storage 160

Gaia 145

George Washington . . 69, 111, 120, 154

Germany . . 16, 20, 42, 46-53, 55-57, 59

Global Warming 29, 63

Gog 71-73

Golitsyn 140, 141

Gore 146, 149

Gulf War 29, 65, 67, 142

Gun 141
Hail 60, 86, 87
Hale-Bopp 33
Heavens .. 11, 23, 26, 32, 33, 69, 70, 77,
84, 85, 93, 103, 105, 137-139,
164
Homosexuality .. 35, 60, 120, 121, 123,
124, 126, 150, 151
Hope.............. 118, 126, 139, 151
Hyakutake 33
Idaho 148
Immigration 143
Iran 73, 154, 163
Iraq 65, 66, 73, 142, 154
Israel . 22, 23, 26, 33, 35, 51, 72, 75, 79,
82, 84, 87, 91, 92, 94-96, 104,
116, 118, 129, 136, 138, 139,
142, 163
Japan 47, 48, 163, 164
Jerusalem .. 9, 10, 25, 26, 29, 32, 46, 59,
71, 76, 77, 79, 81, 83, 84, 89-95,
97, 100, 101, 114, 116, 118, 129-
131, 134-136, 139, 163, 164
Jesus .. 0, v, vi, 1, 2, 4, 5, 7-9, 21, 33, 36-
38, 40, 59, 60, 78, 79, 81, 87, 89,
90, 100, 103-111, 113, 115, 118,
120, 123, 124, 126, 131, 132,
150
John .. 15, 21, 24, 26, 28, 39, 49, 54-56,
58, 61, 62, 64, 65, 67, 70, 82-89,
92, 101, 107-110, 114, 116-118,
151
Kingdom of the Beast .. 15, 46, 79, 150,
151
Libya 71, 73, 163
Lightning 7, 8, 78, 104
Lightning(s) 83, 93
Maitreya..................... 79, 80
Menorah........................ 34
Messiah .. 8, 32, 34, 79, 89, 90, 96, 104,
130, 131
Meteorite 34, 84, 85, 87, 88
Middle East 120

Miracles .. 43-45, 51, 68, 71, 78, 79, 82,
92
Missile 142, 143
Money 44, 53, 143, 150, 158
Montana..................... 148
Moon .. iii, 10, 11, 24, 26, 28, 32-34, 63,
84, 86, 88, 98, 103, 137-139
Moses 8, 23, 32, 59, 78, 81, 87, 96,
111, 118, 162, 164
Mother Earth 126, 161
National Park.............. 147, 148
NATO 73, 141, 142, 144, 154
Naziism 46, 47, 50, 52
Netanyahu 163
Nuclear 51, 62, 120, 142, 164
Oceans 84, 88
Oregon 148, 149
Orion 33
Passover 32-34, 96, 97
Pestilence 29, 72, 87
Plague . 29, 58-68, 70, 79, 81, 83, 86-88,
90, 91, 111, 120, 164
Planet 99, 100, 152
Prayer 126
Prepare .... v, 1, 5, 72, 80, 95, 126, 154,
155, 160
Rabin 163
Recession 165
Red Heifer 94-97, 164
Richard Nixon 146
Rivers 58, 62, 136, 139, 149
Romania..................... 47, 73
Russia 46-48, 51, 62, 73, 154, 163
Sabbath 51, 77, 121, 123
Sara Brady 141
Satan . 36, 38-40, 42, 43, 46, 47, 53, 55,
60, 78, 100, 140, 143
Savior .. vi, 4, 7, 8, 11, 12, 21, 26, 28, 33,
37, 39, 59, 70, 76, 77, 86, 89, 94,
102, 104, 105, 107, 114, 120,
122, 123, 125, 126
Sea ... iii, 11, 28, 32, 41, 44, 58, 59, 61,
69, 84, 88, 93, 97, 116, 118, 126,

136, 138
Silence 103, 104
Sioux 161
Sovereignty 140, 141, 144, 147
Soviet Union 68, 80, 141
Star 32, 62, 64, 88
Storm 72
Sun . . . iii, 10, 11, 24, 26, 28, 32, 34, 58,
         63-65, 86, 88, 92, 98, 101, 103,
         104, 137-139, 159
Sunday . . . . v, 33, 34, 109
Syria 73, 129, 133, 134, 163
Temple 9, 25, 34, 58, 77, 83, 86, 89,
         94-97, 100, 129-131, 134, 135,
         164
Ten Virgins 3-5, 114, 154
THE EVIL KINGDOM OF THE BEAS
         . . . . . T140, 143, 144, 149, 152,
         154, 155
Time Magazine 53, 143
Torah 162
Turkey 20, 73
UN 144-146, 148
UNEP 145, 146
UNESCO 144-146
United Nations . . . 31, 52, 79, 141, 142,
         144, 145, 147, 148, 164
United States . 16, 29, 48, 52, 62, 68-70,
         97, 120, 123, 140-142, 144-147,
         149, 150, 154, 163-165
Virgo 34
Voices 83, 86, 93, 94, 101, 103
Volcano 61
Washington 69, 111, 120, 148, 151,
         154
Weapons 51, 67, 68, 120
Weather 28, 29, 58, 63, 120
Wetlands 149
Wickedness . . 22, 23, 25, 35, 36, 41, 65,
         71, 76, 115, 120, 125, 126, 150
Wilderness Areas 145, 147
Witchcraft 110, 122

Wolves 122, 148
World Heritage 145-147
Wormwood 62, 63
Y2K 152-160
Yellowstone 147-149
Yugoslavia 47, 73